D1624912

Structural Arithmetic Metaphor
in the Oxford "Roland"

Structural
Arithmetic Metaphor
in the Oxford "Roland"

Eleanor Webster Bulatkin

Ohio State University Press

398.2
B933a

Copyright © 1972 by the Ohio State University Press

All rights reserved

International Standard Book Number: 0-8142-0154-7
Library of Congress Catalogue Card Number: 71-141496
Printed in the United States of America

to Iliya Bulatkin
Cossack of the Don

059663

Contents

Illustrations

Introduction

THE DIVINITY which lent its name to the *Divine Comedy* was a triune godhead. For this reason Dante arranged his poem so that, as his reader progressed across the three realms of the Christian cosmos and up through the nine moving spheres of heaven to the empyrean tenth at the apex of all, that divinity implied in his title would be reiterated continually in the triads of the poem's formal divisions as they resolved ceaselessly into unity. Thirty-three cantos of the *Inferno*, thirty-three of the *Purgatorio*, and thirty-three of the *Paradiso* are united into one hundred by the single canto of the introduction, while the *terza rima*, ABA BCD CDC . . . , linking those hendecasyllable lines stressed always on the tenth, insistently restates the all-pervading pattern of the divine Trinity. For Dante, such an arrangement would be fitting because the divine Creator of the comedy which the poem treats was also the God who, according to Solomon, had ordered all things in measure and number and weight.[1] Thus, when Dante ordered his poem in conformity with a numbered pattern, he followed a creative procedure which derived authority from the primeval creative act of God.[2]

Before Dante, in Charlemagne's time, Angilbert had designed

the Centula Abbey at Saint Riquier so that the cloisters formed
a triangle with a church at each angle. One hundred monks
served at each of the three churches, totaling three hundred in
all; and thirty-three children formed the choirs of each—the
whole arranged expressly in honor of the Holy Trinity.[3]

Somewhat later, about the year 1040, but still almost three
centuries before the *Divine Comedy*, the poet who composed the
Old French *Vie de Saint Alexis* arranged his poem in conformity
with an arithmetic scheme based on the powers of five, a number
which, because it represented the sum of 3, the first masculine
number, and 2, the first feminine number, had symbolized marriage since the time of the Pythagoreans. Using a ten-syllable
line with caesura after the fourth, and a five-line stanza, the poet
chose to tell the story of Alexis in 125 stanzas (the third power
of five) or 625 lines (the fourth power of five). Then counting
from the end of the poem, he assigned 125 lines, or 25 stanzas
(the second power of five), to a kind of coda treating the apotheosis of the saint. At this juncture he had remaining 100 stanzas
or 500 lines in which to tell of the saint's life on earth. The block
of 100 stanzas he divided into three equal parts of 33 and $\frac{1}{3}$
stanzas, causing the points of division to fall at crucial points in
the narrative: the moment of the saint's election as the Man of
God (stanza 34, line 170), the moment of his death and ascent
to heaven (stanza 67, line 334), and the moment when his body
is prepared for burial (stanza 100, line 500).

In choosing for the main body of his poem a unit of 100, which
he divided as equally as he could into three parts, the poet of
the *Alexis* expressed in his way the same tripartite division of
unity that Angilbert had attempted in the Centula Abbey and
which Dante later accomplished in the *Divine Comedy*. In all
cases the unity of the Christian Trinity was symbolized; and in
the *Alexis*, the units $33\frac{1}{3}$ would also symbolize the number of
years traditionally ascribed as the span of the life of Christ,
whose example the saint was imitating. Finally, in choosing the
number five as the basis for his overall structure, the *Alexis* poet
restated metaphorically the thematic message which he wished
his poem to convey—in this case, marriage in the sense of the

saint's rejection of earthly marriage for the spiritual union of his soul with God.[4]

Ernst Curtius devotes one of the excurseses of his celebrated work to an exploration of evidence of "numerical composition" prior to Dante, and concludes that, in one way or another, combinations of numbers had been used in the structure of literary works since classical antiquity, at times simply to achieve harmonies and symmetrical proportions, but often to express symbolic meanings as well.[5]

The particular kind of numerical composition with which this study is concerned will be called "structural arithmetic metaphor," a term which may be defined as an ordering of poetic form according to an arithmetic pattern which uses numbers whose symbolic meaning restates metaphorically some basic idea inherent in the content of the poem. The usage of the number five in the *Alexis* would exemplify the procedure. Although no *ars poetica* describing such a device has come down to us, the evidence of the *Alexis* and of Dante's works is sufficient to justify an assumption that the practice was viable at least within the period between the composition of the *Alexis* and the writing of the *Divine Comedy*. It is the purpose of the present work to show that, in addition to its usage in the hagiographic literature of this epoch, the device was also employed for the special type of epic poem represented by the Oxford version of the *Chanson de Roland*.[6] However, since the taste for the manipulation of numbers in literature is no longer viable in modern aesthetics, it will be necessary to discuss the evolution and background of medieval number symbolism before proceeding to the demonstration of its use in the Oxford *Roland*.

---

1. *Biblia Sacra utrisque testamenti* (Palmaguar, 1590), p. 688, Sapientiae, chapter eleven, verse twenty-one: "Sed omnis in mensura et numero et pondere disposuisti." Cf. R. H. Charles, *Apocrypha and Pseudepigrapha of the Old Testament in English* (Oxford, 1913), 1:553, where in the Book of Wisdom, the passage is translated in verse twenty of chapter eleven: "But by measure and number and weight thou didst order all things."

2. See Charles S. Singleton, *An Essay on the Vita Nuova,* and "The Poet's Number at the Center," *MLN* 80 (1965): 1–10, regarding the symbolic numerical structure of the *Vita Nuova* and the *Divina Commedia.*

3. Adolphe Didron, *Christian Iconography: The History of Christian Art in the Middle Ages,* trans. E. J. Millington and Margaret Stokes, 1:61.

4. See Eleanor Webster Bulatkin, "The Arithmetic Structure of the Old-French *Vie de Saint Alexis,*" *PMLA* 74 (1959): 495–502; and Paul G. Imhoff, "The Numerical Symbolism in the Old-French Poem *La Vie de Saint Alexis.*"

5. Ernest Robert Curtius, *European Literature and the Latin Middle Ages,* pp. 501–9.

6. The works known to the writer which have attempted to formulate an arithmetic structure for Digby-23 have been limited to the statement of a possible numerical pattern and do not pretend to integrate the arithmetic device as a metaphoric expression of the sense of the content. C. A. Robson, "The Technique of Symmetrical Composition in Medieval Poetry," in *Studies in Medieval French Presented to Alfred Ewert,* ed. E. A. Francis, pp. 26–70, treats arithmetic divisions in terms of the pagination of Digby-23; and in his master's thesis, "The Mathematical Structure of the *Chanson de Roland,* MS Digby-23," Robert Lucas treats a *schema* based on golden mean proportions in the numbers of the lines and the laisses, and proposes a reading of the line and laisse numbers at variance with that of Paul Mortier's diplomatic edition, *Les Textes de la Chanson de Roland,* vol. 1. In neither case is there overlapping with the present study.

**Structural Arithmetic Metaphor
in the Oxford "Roland"**

The Meaning of Numbers in the Middle Ages

Chapter One

IN THE EVALUATION OF AESTHETIC FUNCTIONS, modern practice tends to distinguish rather sharply between knowing in a cerebral way and perceiving in a sensual way. It is generally felt today that metaphor, or indeed any figurative or symbolic device, should function to bring abstract concepts within the range of human comprehension by making them perceptible to the senses. The usage of a numerical symbol, as the number five is used in the *Vie de Saint Alexis* to express the concept marriage, would constitute a reversal of this process, for the number is an abstraction in itself and symbolic only by reason of an arbitrary, and for us rather silly, assignation of meaning. Furthermore, the number is so buried in the structure of this poem as to be inaccessible to the imagination without recourse to some very cerebral arithmetic calculations. Clearly, the specific medieval point of view which deemed it worthwhile to construct a poem in the manner of the *Alexis* is so far removed from the modern attitude that a frame of reference must be supplied to explain the artistic validity of the procedure.

An examination of the several streams of tradition of which the practice was a product will show to what extent numbers were fundamental realities in the minds of medieval men and how essential they were to any artistic creation that pretended to harmonize with that finite totality which was their world.

Since the history of number symbolism lies somewhat outside of the range of studies on the Old French epic literature, a summary exposition of this topic will be given here, derived in the main from the work of Vincent Hopper, which is one of the most comprehensive studies to date on the subject.[1]

Hopper defines three distinct ways of viewing numbers derived from three major sources which later coalesced into medieval number philosophy (pp. ix, x). The first, which he labels "elementary," is derived from the identification of certain fixed natural groups with their corresponding numbers. A hand would thus be five; a man, twenty (ten fingers and ten toes). The second had its origin in the Babylonian science of astrology, which held in awe as divinely ordained numbers derived from constellations, planets, and stellar revolutions. The third, he traces to the number theory of the Pythagoreans, which "fixed the relationship of the numbers to one another and, accordingly, the places of the astrological aggregates in the Cosmic Order."

Elementary Numerical Associations

As man progressed from that first activity of counting which would be the distinction of *one* from *many* he must surely have isolated the concept *pair* from his observance of the numerous dualities and antitheses of nature: day and night, man and woman, sun and moon, and, at a later stage, perhaps, good and bad. He then had at his command three numerical concepts: 1, 2, and many, and the idea *many* came to be identified with the concept of 3. Hopper suggests that this may have occurred "because 3 is the first integer to which the idea of *many* may be applied, or because . . . the *many* word became incorporated as the third integer in a more advance system" (p. 4). He offers as evidence of this stage of reasoning the singular, dual, and plural, and the positive, comparative, and superlative systems in numerous languages.

Hopper defines the 3 identified with *many* or *all* as the "cumulative" or "statistical" 3 still viable in the logic of modern inductive reasoning: a single occurrence is not significant, a second occurrence may be coincidence, but a third occurrence suggests that a law is in operation. An outgrowth of this half-instinctive mode of reasoning is the rationale of the widely-held superstition that what happens twice must happen a third time (and that will be all) (p. 5). Myth and folklore abound in three wishes, three tries, three suitors.

Perhaps because of the implication of *all* in the statistical 3, perhaps because of numerous simple analogies in the physical and social world, the number three is, according to Hopper, the most ancient and universal number of deity (pp. 6–8). At the suggestion of the family triad, man, woman, and child, and, by extension, of the total idea of generation, parallel celestial families were invented to direct and control matters of generation on earth. Osiris, Isis, and Horus are the most famous of such triads. Observable tripartite divisions of the physical world: heaven, earth, and the underworld; heaven, earth, water; the rising, midday, and setting sun; or spring, summer, and winter, the three divisions of the Indian year; all gave rise to triads or trinities of deities to control each of the threefold domains. The gods of the sky, of the atmosphere and the earth in the Rigveda, the Sumerian Anu, Enlil, and Enki (later Anu, Baal, and Hea), the Greek Zeus, Hades, and Poseidon; the Egyptian Horus, Ra, and Atun are such deities. The concepts of birth, life, and death have produced the Greek fates, Klotho, Lachesis, and Atrapos; the Scandinavian Norns, Urd, Verdandi, and Skuld; and the Indian Brahma, Vishnu, and Siva. Hopper concludes his discussion of the elementary conception of 3 with the observation that, at the dawn of history the number "had already robed itself in manifold meanings, and bore a ruling and godly aspect from which man was not soon to escape" (p. 8).

According to Hopper, the concept of the number four had its origin in the dawning awareness of the four directions: toward the sunrise and the sunset and then toward the points of the verticals to the path of the sun (pp. 8, 9). The conception of the four winds would naturally follow, and the widespread prevalence among primitive cultures of the equal armed cross, the swastika, and other cruciform emblems lends credence to the theory as do also the supports of the heavenly roof in the figures of four mountains, four pillars, or the four women of Egyptian cosmogony. In any event the idea of the "fourness" of earth is such a universal commonplace that its origins must also have occurred in that elementary stage of arithmetic reasoning when the concrete associations of number were more real than abstract.

For modern arithmetic, by far the most significant advance in the associational stage of arithmetic reasoning was the discovery that the fingers and toes could be used as counting devices. As a far-reaching consequence of this ancient realization, the decimal system of counting was born, where, as Hopper observes, the integers of the decade take on the semblance of immortal essences, and the possibility of infinite repetition of digits provides for infinite variation of fundamental number symbols (pp. 9, 10).

He notes as an interesting example of usage of decimal counting to determine literary form, the numeration of the twenty-eight poems of the so-called *Thousand Songs of Thebes* of ca. 1300 B.C. The poems are numbered from 1 to 10 and then 20, 30, 40, etc. to 100 and then by hundreds to chapter 1,000, which is actually the 28th chapter.[2] Hopper continues: "Every member of the decade is thereby repeated 3 times and the contents of chapter 80, for example, will be found to refer to the sanctity of the number 8." A very early figurative usage of the repeated digit is to be found on a Cainite tablet which states that "if Cain is avenged 7-fold then Lamech 70 and 7."[3] "Centuries later," Hopper continues (pp. 9, 10): "Thomas Aquinas [*Expositio II* in *Apocalypsium* 14] in his solution of 666, the number of the beast in Revelations, discusses 6 in relation to unity, 6 in relation to the denarius, and 6 in relation to the hundred."

It is of special import to the present study to note that the concept of the repeated digit on which Saint Thomas relies for his interpretation of 666 would have received reinforcement from the columnal decimal system of notation which, by his time, was well established in Europe through the use of the abacus. An improvement on this ancient device was invented by the mathematician Gerbert (956–1003), who was to become Pope Sylvester II, and who taught at Bobbio and Reims. Gerbert's invention comprised a board divided into thirty columns, three being reserved for fractions, while the remaining 27 were divided into groups of three columns each, designated S (singularis), D (decem), and C (centum). Addition, subtraction, and multiplication were carried out very much as today by simply placing disks marked with signs for numerals in the appropriate column. Thus a 4 in the S column would mean 4, in the D column, 40, and in the C column, 400, and so forth. No zero was necessary.[4]

Naturally, in a decimal system the number ten as the symbol of the entire method of numeration achieves importance in itself and acquires connotations of completeness and finality, as do its multiples, one hundred and one thousand. The case of the *Thousand Songs of Thebes*, cited previously, stands as an expression of such feeling in literary form as do the ten books of hymns celebrating the chief gods in the Rigveda. In the Judeo-Christian world, the Ten Commandments of the Old Testament have conferred divine authority on the number.

It would be natural also to expect that since the idea of completeness is conveyed by 10, the number nine would suggest "almost completeness" and the number eleven, "excess." Hopper cites as an example of the former the 9–10 relationship in the *Iliad* and the *Odyssey*, where Troy, beseiged for nine years, fell on the tenth; and where Odysseus wandered for nine years to return home on the tenth (p. 10). The evolution of the concept of 11 as the number of excess is of special import to the present study and will be treated in detail in a later section.

Hopper concludes that, although in more sophisticated epochs the numbers which have been discussed may receive additional connotations, their elementary meanings are seldom lost: 3 is "all" (beginning, middle, and end), "best" (superlative), "holy" (triads of gods); 4 is the number of earth; 10 is completeness and perfection; and 9 is all but complete (p. 11).

Astronomical Associations

The pattern of thought which associates number with the observable groups of the everyday world extends naturally to association with the movements of the heavenly bodies. However, since such movements seem to be ordered and controlled by unseen powers, the numbers observable in them take on the qualities of devine essences empowered by active forces. The essences then become objects of worship in themselves and the knowledge and manipulation of them becomes a special prerogative of the controlling gods and their priests. Thus, as Hopper mentions, the supreme secret which the Babylonian god Ea taught to his son was called the "number" and the goddess Nisaba is characterized as "she who knows the significance of numbers and carries the tablet of the stars" (p. 12).[5]

The most easily observed of the celestial movements would obviously have been the cycle of lunations; and the four periods of the moon's phases—waxing half, full, waning half, dark— would reiterate the elementary quaternity of earth and give prominence to a division of time into four periods of seven days each, which doubtless accounts for the fact that the seven-day week is universally the most prevalent. That the seventh day came to have a baleful aspect is attested in a Babylonian calendar mentioned by Hopper which lists as evil days the seventh, fourteenth, twenty-first, twenty-eighth, and also the nineteenth, which is the forty-ninth (7 x 7) from the first of the preceding thirty-day month (p. 13). Thus, in resting from the labors of creation on the seventh day, the Hebrew Jahveh acted in conformity with the Babylonian tradition of the baleful seventh.[6]

The observations by shepherds and navigators of the seven stars in the Bear and the Pleïades, surely gave further prominence to the number seven. Hopper maintains that the seven stars of the Bear, the constellation visible throughout the year, probably provided the pattern for the seven gods of the Brahmanas who preceded the flood and the seven wise ones saved after the flood who wrote down the secrets of devination, magic, and wisdom, as well as for the seven Hathors of Egypt, the seven seers of Vedic ritual, and the seven sages of Greece (p. 15). He concludes that seven thus became, in one aspect, "a number of wisdom and godliness."

Of far-reaching significance to the number mysticism of even modern times was the descent of the seven stars of the Pleïades below the horizon for forty days every year, for this period coincided with the rainy season in ancient Babylon and was a time of storm, flood, and general tribulation, all attributed to the exile of the beneficent stars. The understanding of forty as a number of exile is reflected in the forty years of Hebrew wandering in the desert, the forty days spent by Moses on Mount Sinai, and the forty days of Lent, and is viable today in the word *quarantine*, which stems from the forty-day period of isolation in the port of Rome. Another result of the descent of the Pleïades was the attribution of evil significance to the number seven, for while the seven stars were absent, they were cursed for their merciless and destructive influence.

The special import of the manifold connotations of the number seven to the argument of the present work will be discussed in detail later. For the present, it will suffice to note that the ambivalent feelings with regard to the number, originating in the ambience of man's earliest astronomical observations, flourish in abundance in the Old Testament. Perhaps the most striking exemplification of the good and bad qualities of the number seven is to be found in Genesis 41, where Pharaoh dreams of seven fat kine and seven good ears of corn swallowed up by seven lean kine and seven thin ears. Joseph interpreted the dream to mean seven years of plenty followed by seven years of famine in Egypt. From the concept of the rest of Jahveh on the seventh day, there arose the idea of the six ages of the world comprising six days of a thousand years plus a seventh of eternal rest. In the genealogies of the descendants of Adam, the number seven is prominent in both the good line and the bad. Thus, seven names are mentioned in the line from Cain to Lamech, who lived 777 years, and it is stated in Genesis 4:24 that "if Cain be avenged 7 fold, truly Lamech shall be avenged 70 and 7." The good Enoch, however, is also the seventh in the genealogical tree, and the tree of life of seven branches with seven leaves each became the seven branched candlestick of the Hebrew menora. The righteous in Israel are named as 7,000, there are seventy nations, seventy children of Jacob, and seventy judges of Sanhedrun.

The eighth day, conceived as a day of plenty after fasting or purification after cleanliness, is also the day of circumcision, and after a period of 7 x 7 or 49 years, the fifieth is holy.

Hopper remarks that "probably the earliest year was that of 12 lunations with a 13th month later intercalated from time to time, this carrying with it an inauspicious and baleful aspect" (p. 19). In any event, he maintains that twelve signs of the zodiac were discovered as the appointed rulers of the months and that twelve stars selected as objects for devotion soon were doubled to a set for the Northern Hemisphere and one for the Southern, following the principal of the dualism of good and evil. An expansion of the pattern and similar dualistic reasoning led to the establishment of two sets of twelve divisions for the hours of the day and the night. The twenty-four stars of the Northern and Southern Hemispheres became the twenty-four judges of the living and the dead who perhaps live on in the twenty-four elders of the Book of Revelation.

Hopper points out that duodecads have been prominent in every ancient civilization and cites as examples the twelve spokes in the wheel of the Hindu Rta, the twelve gates of hell where Egyptian Ra must spend the twelve hours of night, the twelve tribes of Israel, the twelve labors of Hercules, the twelve gods of Greece and of Rome, and the twelve tables of Roman law (p. 21). Obviously, through its association with temporal divisions, the number receives prominence in the Old Testament in the ordering of administrative functions. Thus David (I Chronicle 24:25) divides the sons of Aaron into twenty-four orders so that no hour of the day or night be neglected, and twelve captains are appointed (one for each month), each ruling over 24,000 men.

To what extent the prevalence of the duodecads is related to the duodecadial system of counting practiced by the Babylonians and Chaldeans is a subject worthy of consideration. This system based on twelve units, which survives today in the division of the circle into 360 degrees, is much more flexible than our decimal system, for since the number twelve is divisible by two, three, four, and six, it can be fractioned into a half, a third, a quarter, and a sixth. In contrast, a system based on ten digits can only be divided by two and five, or fractioned into the half and fifth. The survival of remnants of the duodecadial system into the Middle Ages (and into modern times, for that matter) has, when it comes into conflict with the prevailing decimal system, produced some amusing arithmetic dilemmas. As will later become apparent, the unwieldy decimal system posed insoluble paradoxes when Christian number philosophy attempted to derive the Trinity from unity. Without a workable system for the notation of fractions, it is simply impossible to divide one or ten or one hundred, and so forth into three parts.[7]

Hopper suggests that a new stage in the history of number symbolism was inaugurated in the later apocalyptic writings of the Hebrews, which sought in the great astrological numbers such as four, seven, and twelve, interrelations which would serve as fundamental patterns on which prognoses of the future could be based (p. 30). Thus, the quarternity of earth, as evident in the cardinal points, winds, seasons, phases of the moon, and so forth, was conceived as a manifestation in the observable microcosm of an archetypal pattern in the macrocosm and justification for the assumption that four is the number of earth, time, and life in this world. The significance of such numbers was felt to be occasionally perceptible to a highly devout elite but completely knowable only to God. Thus, St. John, endowed with such perception, can say (Revelation 7:4) : "And I heard the number of them that were sealed: and there were sealed 144,000 [i.e., an extension of 12 x 12] of all the tribes of the children of Israel."

Pythagorean Numbers

While the symbolism of the astrological numbers was being elaborated in Africa, on the north shore of the Mediterranean a somewhat different way of considering numbers seems to have originated independently in the sixth century B.C. among the adherents of the cult of mystic philosophy led by Pythagoras.[8] Little is certainly known about Pythagoras or his followers, and the information we have regarding their number theory comes to us through the comments of Plato and Aristotle and later philosophers. The so-called Pythagoreanism known to the Middle Ages is in fact that corpus of mathematical writing by the Neo-Pythagoreans, who, between the first century B.C. and the fifth century A.D., perpetuated the tradition of the now vanished writings of their predecessors which they had received through Plato. Such men were: Philo the Jew, Nicomachus of Gerasa, and Plutarch, of the first century A.D.; Plotinus, Diogenes Laertius, Porphyry, and Iamblicus, of the third century; and Proclus, Macrobius, and Capella, of the fifth century.

According to Hopper, the two principles of Pythagoreanism most influential in medieval number philosophy were the *exultation of the decade* as containing all numbers and therefore all things and the *geometric conception of numerical relations* (p. 34). Perhaps the most succinct (if not entirely sympathetic) statement of their mathematical philosophy is that which Hopper cites from Aristotle's *Metaphysica* A.5:

> The first to take up mathematics . . . [the Pythagoreans] thought its principles were the principles of all things. Since of these principles numbers are by nature the first, and in number they seem to see many resemblances to the things that exist and come into being . . . since again they saw that the modifications and ratios of the musical scales were expressible in numbers . . . they supposed the elements of number to be the elements of all things, and the whole heavens to be a musical scale and number. And all the properties of numbers and scales which they could show to agree with the attributes and parts of the whole arrangement of the heavens, they collected and fitted into their scheme, and if there was a gap anywhere, they readily made additions so as to make their whole theory coherent.[9]

Aristotle's skepticism was evidently prompted by the Pythagorean cosmic theory which posited a universe comprising a central fire around which revolve earth, sun, moon, planets, and the six stars, resulting in a total of nine spheres, to which they added an invisible counterearth to bring the number to the completeness of the decade. (In the light of modern science, where mathematics has so often led to discovery—Mendeleev's table of atomic weights would be a case in point— the reasoning of the Pythagoreans does not seem so faulty!)

The geometric conception of numbers provided the link between their abstract and concrete qualities. The number one was conceived as the point; and the number two, since it could be viewed as extension between two points, was equated with the line. The number three, then, was seen as the triangle; and, since this configuration was the first in the series with concrete form, the triangle was held to be the basis of all perceptible objects, and the number three was thus called the first real number. Then, since four points can be construed in a pyramid, the number four was called the first solid and, through the suggestions of its shape, was also equated with fire. The first four numbers were thus conceived as the archetypal numbers since by means of them the point, line, surface, and solid could be represented.

Reasoning from the arithmetic and geometric qualities of numbers, the Pythagoreans then proceeded to endow them with philosophic properties. The monad was deemed the first principle from which all other numbers flow and, since its figuration was simply a point and not a construct perceptible to the senses, was considered an essence rather than a being. It was called the father of number and equated to God as the basis and creator of numbers. In it were combined the qualities of both odd and even, and male and female, for when added to odd numbers it produces even, and to even, odd. Although called the great Even-Odd it was, nevertheless, considered more odd (good) than even (not good).

In similar vein the number two was called the mother of numbers but, like one, was deemed to be a principle rather than a number because, as in the case of the point, the line is not concrete. The number two, however, stood lower in the hierarchy of philosophic quantities than the great monad, for it was felt to have the somewhat negative properties of diversity, separation from unity, and, because it was divisible, mutability. It was held to be more nearly related to matter and existence and thus not equated with essence or idea, and it was associated with the notion of excess and defect.

A set of oppositions embodied in the first principles, one and two, ran somewhat as follows: the monad was held to represent the intelligible, the immortal, the right side, the day, the east, the sun, and equality, while the duad was associated with the sensible, the mortal, the left side, the night, the west, the moon, and inequality.

Since limit and unity were desiderata in the Pythagorean system, the numbers following after the first two principles were generally considered good or bad, depending on whether they were odd or even. Even numbers were called feminine because they were "empty in the center" and always divisible. Therefore, they were the weaker. Odd numbers were called masculine and considered the "masters" of the feminine "slaves," since, when added to even, they always produced odd. The even numbers were, because of their divisibility, generally associated with the infinite, a concept rather repulsive to Greek thought, while the odd connoted finite limits, rest, and completeness. The fact that the progression of the odd numbers from the monad always produces squares (i.e., one plus three equals four, plus five equals nine, plus seven equals sixteen, etc.) no doubt served to further enhance the esteem in which they were held within this system of reasoning.

Three, the first real number and the first of the masculine, finite, and God-like odd numbers, was felt to symbolize all reality, that is, the beginning, the middle, and the end. It restores to harmony the unity of one and the diversity of 2 of which it is the sum, linking them by this means into a single and complete order. In the logic of the Pythagorean triad can be seen the basic philosophy of the Christian Trinity, and in the fifth century of our era we find Proclus maintaining (*Elements of Theology* 50.148) that "every divine order has an internal unity of three-fold origins from its highest, its mean, and its last term."

The tetrad as the last of archetypal numbers was viewed with special favor because it produces the decade, either as the sum (one plus two plus three plus four equals ten), or as the number of points in the sides of the figured representation of ten as a triangular number.

In the Pythagorean system, the numbers five and six were both associated with the idea of marriage as being either the sum or the product of the first feminine 2 and the first masculine 3; and, as would naturally be supposed, the number five, being odd, was considered the masculine marriage number, while the even number six was the feminine and was indeed called the number of Venus by Capella (*De Nuptiis* 7). Worthy of note is the fact that it is in the fifth book of the *Republic* that Plato speculates so extensively on the properties of the "marriage number," which is apparently derived from the 3, 4, 5, right triangle, whose hypothenuse was 5 and whose area was 6!

Plato (*Timaeus* 38) designates the number seven as the "moveable image of eternity." Seven was also deemed to be the virgin number, since it neither generates (a square, cube, etc.) nor is generated within the decade. Thus, by reason of its isolation, it shared somewhat the respect ascribed to unity and bore fittingly the weight of symbolic meaning which it had received through astrological associations as a great lunar number, since the sum of the first seven numbers equals 28—the number of days of the lunar cycle! It was also known as the number of harmony and, through its association with the seven tones of the musical scale, the seven vowels, and the seven stars of the Pleïade, was called by Plutarch the "lyre of the muses" (*Sur l'E de Delphes* 4).

The special reverence reserved for the number ten derives, of course, from the fact that, in the decimal system of counting, all other digits are incorporated in it; and it seems to represent a kind of resolution of multiplicity into a higher order of unity. Porphyry calls it comprehension because it comprehends "all differences of numbers, reason, species, and proportions." The multiples of ten by itself (100, 1,000, and so forth) were called the "boundaries" of number with similar unifying properties ascribed to them; and, since all higher numbers are generated by the members of the decade, they were felt to derive their special qualities from their unit progenitors.

The Pythagoreans had little quarrel with either the traditional elementary or the astronomical significances of numbers, and the fact that the two concepts could be easily harmonized can be seen in the manner in which the arithmetic properties of 7 were found to be in accord with its astronomical association. Similarly, the philosophic logic of the triad was but a reiteration of the age-old elementary association of three with the idea of all deity as comprising beginning, middle, and end.

Transmission to the Middle Ages

Such in outline was the vast body of numerical lore which Western civilization had at its disposition at the dawn of the Christian era: an accumulation of beliefs and associations stemming from that first awareness of the difference between the one and the many in the prehistory of man's thought which gathered acretions from his observations of phenomena in the heavens and in the world in which he found himself and which received final sanction from his inquiries into the nature and combining properties inherent in the numbers themselves.

Hopper stresses the fact that perhaps the most influential figure in the transmission of this lore to the culture of Western Christendom was Philo the Jew, that great scholar of biblical exegesis whose writings in the first century after Christ established the principle of allegorical interpretation of the Hebrew scriptures and were to serve as the model of biblical commentary not only for the Jews, but for all of the fathers of the Christian church, both Greek and Roman (pp. 46–49).

Philo was essentially an Alexandrian who believed that the physical world was a manifestation of the ideas inherent in the Logos, that great depository of all the patterns of all the forms. The world perceptible to the senses was for him a kind of "forest of the symbols," a metaphor used by both Origen and Baudelaire, whose true meaning can be known by analyzing correspondences or the allegorical significance of the perceived manifestations. Allegorical exegesis of the sensible world is thus the way back to essence from appearance, and number is especially helpful in this procedure, for as Plotinus says (*Enneades* 6.6.4-5) "number exists before objects which are described by number." Number, then, was a sort of window in the sensory world through which the essence of the patterns in the Logos could be perceived. (Solomon, whose wisdom was being recorded at about the time of Philo, is thus presumed to have said that God disposed all in number and measure and weight.)

Within this pattern of reasoning then, Philo was justified in seeking a message in the numbers of the Hebrew scripture and for applying in his interpretations all the baggage of symbolic meaning which previous cultures had handed down to him. Thus, when he found what seemed to be Pythagorean elements in the books of Moses, it was natural for him to conclude, as Hopper notes, that the Greeks had gotten their learning from these books at an earlier age (p. 47). In this manner divine authority, which had hitherto been limited to the astrological numbers, was now conferred on Pythagoreanism.

Philo combed the scriptures line by line for significant numbers, and none seemed to have been too complicated for his ingenuity to reduce to the archetypal principles. The early Christians, meanwhile, in their simplicity and directness, seemed unconcerned with the sophisticated manipulations of number symbols, but did unwittingly contribute to their propagation by finding in the writings of the Old Testament foreshadowings and prophecies which gave support to the divinity of Jesus as a long awaited Messiah.[10] The doctrine of the fulfillment of the scriptures made it inevitable that units of time and patterns of numbers which had persisted through the old records be repeated in the recordings of the new events. Thus, it was only natural that, for example, the number of days of Christ's temptation should be stated as forty after the model of the forty days of Elija's solitude, the forty days of trial by flood, and the forty years of Hebrew wandering, and so forth.

Later, when the Christian community attracted to its fold men of scholarly and philosophical leaning, these minds, bent on the creation of a consistent body of Christian theology, naturally operated in the manner suggested by the ambience replete with philosophic interest in numbers in which they were nurtured. Such were Clement of Alexandria and his pupils Origen and Hippolytus, as well as Irenaeus, Tertullian, Justin Martyr, and Ambrose. These men, following the lead of Philo, began to write allegorical exegeses of the biblical texts and to interpret the numbers in accordance with all the information at their disposition.

Of paramount importance were problems concerning the numerical composition of the godhead, a matter which seems to have bothered the first-century Christians not at all but which later, under the threat of the Arian heresy, gave promise of splitting the religious construct into an ambivalent duality. A subordinating, yet unifying, readjustment in the Father and Son concept was badly needed, and a great step toward the accomplishment of it was the identification of the Son with the Logos which Philo had posited. The final resolution of the problem was attained, however, with the statement of the Trinity, in which the Holy Ghost would participate as the Third Person, together with the Father and the Son. No doubt the solution was a happy one for the men of that age as well as for those of ages to come, for the idea of a Trinity was consonant with the ambience of Pythagorean distrust of duality and reverence for the triad as a second kind of unity; and, in general, the construct satisfied the universal human compulsion to expect after two an inevitable three of completeness and finality. It also had the practical advantage of providing a replacement with minimal disruption for the age-old triads of gods, whose followers were soon to be converts to the new religion.

The fact that God created the world in six days and rested on the seventh had occasioned much speculation by Philo, who reasoned that 6 was a perfect number "since it is the first number which is equal in its parts, in the half, and the third, and sixth parts [that is, it equals the sum of its divisors three, two, and one] and since it is produced by the multiplication of two unequal factors, two and three. And the numbers two and three exceed the incorporality which exists in the unity because the number two is an image of matter being divided into two parts and dissected like matter. And the number three is an image of a solid body, because a solid can be divided according to a three-fold division."[11]

Mortal beings were thus measured by the number six, and the blessed and immortal by the number seven, which God sanctified by making his seventh creation that of light. Hopper summarizes Philo's remarks in the *Creation* on the sacred number seven, noting that the prominence of this number is explained by its archetypal position as "lord of the universe," the image of God "being one, eternal, lasting, immovable, himself like to himself, and different from all other beings" (p. 48).

The analogy of the creation led to much speculation regarding the duration of the world and, starting with the statement in the ninetieth psalm that a day with the Lord is as 1,000 years, that interval was established as the length of the age. There was fairly general agreement among the early fathers that the limit of the world would be 6,000 years, but the fact that Christ was resurrected on the eighth day, that is, the day after the seventh, occasioned some consternation which ultimately was resolved by Augustine, who reasoned that, after the six earthly ages, the seventh day of rest symbolized the culminating Eternal Rest, which would have no evening. The eighth day, then, represented a return to original life, not taken away, but made eternal (Hopper, p. 77).

Indeed, it remained for Augustine to give that final approval of number symbolism which was needed for its perpetuation in Western Christendom. "Augustine is everywhere fascinated by the properties of number," remarks Hopper (p. 79), who cites from the *City of God* 11.30: "We must not despise the science of numbers, which, in many passages of the holy scripture, is found to be of eminent service to the careful interpreter. Neither has it been without reason numbered among God's praises 'Thou hast ordered all things in number, and measure, and weight.'"

Hopper cites at length from Augustine's interpretation of the flood legend in the *Contra Faustum* 12.38 to provide an example of his ingenuity in allegorical exegeses (pp. 80, 81). A part of his citation is given here to show the kind of model for the manipulation of number symbolism which the medieval poets and architects and artists had before them as guides for their own artistic creation.

Omitting, therefore, many passages in these Books, where Christ may be found, but which require longer explanation and proof, although the most hidden meanings are the sweetest, convincing testimony may be obtained from the enumeration of such things as the following: — That Enoch, the 7th from Adam, pleased God, and was translated, as there is to be a 7th day of rest into which all will be translated, who, during the 6th day of the world's history, are created anew by the incarnate Word. That Noah with his family, is saved by water and wood, as the family of Christ was saved by Baptism, as representing the suffering of the Cross. That this ark is made of beams formed in a square, as the Church is constructed of saints prepared unto every good work; for a square stands firm on any side. That the length is 6 times the breadth and 10 times the height, like a human body [prostrate], to show that Christ appeared in a human body. That the breadth reaches to 50 cubits; as the apostle says, "Our heart is enlarged" (II Corinthian vi.2), that is, with spiritual love, of which he says again, "The love of God is shed abroad in our hearts by the Holy Ghost, which is given unto us" (Romans v.5). For in the 50th day after his resurrection, Christ sent his Spirit to enlarge the hearts of his disciples. That it is 300 cubits long, to make up 6 times 50; as there are 6 periods in the history of this world . . . that it is, 30 cubits high, a 10th part of the length; because Christ is one height, who, in his 30th year gave his sanction to the doctrine of the gospel, by declaring that He came, not to destroy the law, but to fulfill it. Now the 10 commandments are known to be the heart of the law; and so the length of the Ark is 10 times 30. Noah himself, too, was the 10th from Adam.

It should not now be difficult for us to imagine that the medieval poet, with such examples before him, would be constrained to imitate in the microcosm of his poems, those creative procedures which, as he had learned, God had used to produce the great macrocosm. Of first order in importance would be a structure or a kind of armature composed of numbers which bore some relation to the import of the story he planned to tell, for he was imbued with the idea that number exists before objects which are described by number, and that in the great creation, as he had learned from Nicomachus in his *Introduction to Arithmetic* 1.6. 1–2, "the pattern was set like a preliminary sketch by the domination of number preexistent in the mind of the world-creating God." Whether or not the numbers would be discernible to his audience was of no importance to such a poet. What must have only mattered to him was his knowledge that, since the thing he wished to create had been made in the proper manner, it would be good, and in harmony with all creation.

1. Vincent Foster Hopper, *Medieval Number Symbolism.* See also Guy Beaujouan ("Le symbolisme des nombres à l'époque romaine, "*Cahiers de civilization médiévale* 4 [1961]: 159–69), who reviews briefly some unedited, twelfth-century tracts on numerical symbolism which were unknown to Hopper. Beaujouan mentions specifically the *Analytica numerorum* of Eudes de Morimond (d. 1161), of MS lat. 3352ᴬ of the Bibliothèque Nationale, and the *De sacramentis numerorum a ternario usque ad duodenarium* (completed between 1165 and 1170) by Guillaume d'Auberive and Geoffroy d'Auxerre, which is to be found in Luxembourg MS 60 along with a similar tract by a certain Thibaud de Langres. Karl Menninger, *Number Words and Number Symbols,* treats the subject from the point of view of language and signs. The book of Christopher Butler, *Number Symbolism* (London, 1970) could not be examined before this work went to press.

2. Hopper cites Adolf Erman, *The Literature of the Ancient Egyptians,* pp. 293–302.

3. Hopper cites H. P. Smith, *Old Testament History,* p. 24.

4. See Florian Cajori, *A History of Mathematics,* pp. 84–137; and Jacques Boyer, *Historie des mathématiques,* pp. 63–87.

5. Hopper cites Charles Victor McLean, *Babylonian Astrology and its Relation to the Old Testament,* p. 22.

6. Hopper cites Hutton Webster, *Rest Days: A Study in Early Law and Morality,* pp. 223, 232; R. Campbell Thompson, *Semitic Magic, Its Origin*

and Development, p. 138; and Maurice H. Farbridge, *Studies in Biblical and Semitic Symbolism*, p. 135.

7. See Bartel Leendert van der Waerden, *Science Awakening*, pp. 37–61, 82–104, et passim.

8. Hopper treats Pythagorean number theory in detail in chapter 3, pp. 31–49.

9. Aristotle, *Metaphysics*, pp. 64, 65.

10. Hopper treats the early Christian approach to numbers in chapter 5, pp. 69–88.

11. *On the Allegories of the Sacred Law* 2, as cited by Hopper, pp. 47, 48.

The Numerical Structures in the Oxford "Roland"

Chapter Two

IN THE YEAR 1053, when the relics of Saint Wolfram were transferred to the abbey of Fontenelle, a canon of Rouen was cured of blindness by their miraculous power as they were carried through the streets. The canon was known as Tedbalt of Vernon and is described as one who translated into the common tongue from Latin the acts of many saints, among them those of Saint Wandrille. It is especially noted that he reworked these *gestes* with artistry and that he made pleasing songs of them to a sort of *tinnuli rhythmi*.[1] The fact that language and other evidence in the *Vie de Saint Alexis* suggest that this work was composed about the year 1040 has prompted the assumption that Tedbalt de Vernon could have been the author of the poem. In any event, the description of Tedbalt's work stands as evidence that, at the period of the composition of the *Alexis*, the deeds of saints were being related in the vernacular as songs in a form with some kind of resounding or tintinabulating rhythm. If by the expression *tinnuli rhythmi* is meant the sort of structural arithmetic metaphor which has been revealed in the *Alexis*, then it may be said that the device was employed for hagiographic material at least on more than one occasion during the first half of the eleventh century.

Since the customary repertory of the early jongleurs comprised songs of both the lives of saints and the deeds of heroes, one might well inquire whether a similar poetic device was employed for epic poetry.[2] For several reasons the obvious choice for testing would be the Oxford version of the *Chanson de Roland*.

It is, of course, widely known that Joseph Bédier and those scholars who were his followers in the 1920s considered Digby-

23, the Oxford manuscript of the *Roland,* to be the oldest and best of all the manuscripts. They also held the version represented in this manuscript to be the original one and maintained that it was composed out of whole cloth at the beginning of the twelfth century by a single individual who was a very gifted poet.[3] However, evidence which has been brought to light in the past few decades has led contemporary scholars more and more to the view that the Oxford version is simply one link of a long chain of reworkings of the material which dates back to the ninth century.[4]

Of the two main episodes of the Oxford *Roland,* only the events of one, that treating the defeat of Charlemagne's army at Roncevaux, stems from a nucleus of historic fact. Charlemagne's rearguard was indeed exterminated at Roncevaux in the year 778, and, by the year 829, the story was already being recounted with characteristic legendary accretions, the most notable being the inclusion of the protagonist Roland, who dies in the battle.[5] The other episode, telling of Charlemagne's battle of vengeance with the Saracen emir Baligant, has no basis in Carolingian history, the material seeming rather to be related to the expedition of Robert Guiscard against Alexis Commenius in 1085.[6]

Present-day scholars are in fairly general agreement that the Roncevaux episode reflected in the Oxford version was completed during the period between the end of the tenth century and quite certainly by 1087, but more likely before 1050. The Baligant episode is considered to be the addition of a later revision which was probably completed between the years 1087 and 1098.[7] Thus, the version of the Oxford manuscript is now believed to be the product of at least two revisions, of which the earliest, comprising the Roncevaux episode, was roughly coetaneous with the composition of the *Vie de Saint Alexis.*

Therefore, the two poems, the *Alexis* and the Roncevaux episode of the Oxford version, would be products of the same period. The possibility of origin in a similar cultural ambience is not lessened by the fact that both poems are in assonanted decasyllable with caesura after the fourth (the so-called "epic" line), the

Alexis being arranged in five-line stanzas, while the *Roland* is in the usual epic laisses of undetermined length. Also, both Digby-23 and manuscript *L* of the *Alexis* are by Anglo-Norman scribes of the twelfth century.[8]

The similarity of the structural effect in the two works is notable, and the fact that both poems exhibit an unusually architectonic form is remarked by all readers. The "genius" of Digby-23 is generally acclaimed; and, with respect to the poem's composition, the version of this manuscript is deemed unique in the vast corpus of French epic material. Since in large measure the form of the *Alexis* is determined by the arithmetic pattern which serves as its armature and since both poems give the impression of carefully planned composition, there would be a good chance that some arithmetic scheme was also used for the *Roland* —a probability which would be heightened by the contemporaneity and similarities of provenience and metric form which have been noted.[9] It would seem, therefore, that, if structural arithmetic metaphor is to be found in any Old French epic poetry, the Oxford version of the *Chanson de Roland* would be a good place to look for it.

The Unity of the Oxford "Roland"

In spite of the fact that the story of Roland and Charlemagne related in Digby-23 represents a combination of two episodes which are historically unconnected, the version as a whole manifests a reasonable degree of artistic unity. Essentially, the defeat of Charlemagne's rearguard at Roncevaux may be described as a tragedy resulting from the interaction of two forces: the one, a plot of betrayal implemented by the traitor Ganelon; the other, the excessive valor of the hero. Positive action on the part of Charlemagne in the developments leading to the tragedy seems rather conspicuous in its absence. Indeed, the king's ineptitude before the decision of his council in the naming of Roland to the rearguard, and his literal absence from the battle through Roland's failure to summon him, might well be considered a third factor of the tragedy.

If the events succeeding the death of Roland are conceived as a sequel to the battle of Roncevaux, then the part of the narrative telling of Charlemagne's battle with Baligant and the trial of Ganelon falls into place as a kind of tailpiece to accommodate the vengeance for the evil action: vengeance on the pagans and justice for the traitor, forcefully executed now by Charlemagne, the very person whose earlier inaction had contributed to the Roncevaux defeat.

The 66 Pattern: Arithmetic Structure

Paul Mortier's diplomatic edition of the Oxford manuscript contains 291 assonanted groups of 10-syllable lines.[10] The number of lines in each group, or laisse, varies at random, the average being fourteen, with a maximum of thirty-five and a minimum of five. Mortier reads 4002 lines in the total.

Obvious divisions of the numbers 291 or 4002 into thirds, quarters, fifths, and so forth do not strike points of outstanding importance in the narrative, and no arithmetic correlation is evident between the 291 laisses and the 4002 lines in the poem, as is the case with the *Alexis*, where the 125 regular five-line stanzas represent the third power of five and, necessarily, the 625 lines represent the fourth. Furthermore, the fact that the number of lines in the laisses of the *Roland* is undetermined renders the probability very high that lines have been lost or added through scribal error, so that, even if originally there had been numerical pattern in the lines, the chances of recovering it now would be slight.[11] Thus, to find an arithmetic plan in the *Roland*, the best procedure would seem to be to disregard the possibility of its presence in line numbers and to hunt for pieces of pattern in the arrangement of the laisses.

Since the number structure of the *Alexis* depends on significant points in the narrative, it would seem logical to choose some focal point in the *Roland* story and then to measure the distance in terms of laisses between that point and subsidiary points. In the *Alexis,* the moment when the saint dies serves as a sort of axis.[12] The death of Roland occurs in laisse 176 of Mortier's edition, and it seems significant that this event is predicted in laisse 110 by a storm and eclipse of the sun over all of France. It will be noted that these narrative points are 66 laisses apart. Assuming for the moment that the bracket of 66 laisses is an intentional structural unit, a count of 66 laisses back from laisse 110 comes to laisse 44, in which Ganelon describes to Marsile the exact details of his plan for the attack on the rearguard and the downfall of Roland. The set of points thus established tells a succinct story of betrayal and destruction: the Plan of Betrayal at 44, the Prediction of Death resulting from the plan at 110, and the Death of Roland itself at 176. (See figure 1.)[13]

Since Roland's companion Olivier, thematically the counterfoil of wisdom and prudence to Roland's proud valor, dies with Roland in the final debacle, the point of his death might also have structural importance. This event occurs in laisse 150, and a count back from 150 by the assumed structural unit of 66 arrives at laisse 84, the middle of three parallel laisses where the famous dispute over the blowing of the horn takes place. Here Olivier advises Roland to sound his horn so that Charles and the main body of the army can come back to rescue them, but Roland refuses because it would be cowardly to seek assistance against the pagans and his name would be disgraced forever in France. This is Roland's act of *démesure,* which, originating in the excessive fortitude universally characteristic of heroes, acts as a sort of tragic flaw which becomes a second factor of his downfall and that of 20,000 men.

A further count of 66 laisses back from the 84th comes to laisse 18, where Olivier speaks for the first time. Charles has asked his council of vassals to name someone for the hazardous and diplomatically demanding mission to the court of the pagan king, Marsile. Roland volunteers, but Olivier rushes forth and asks to be sent in place of his friend, explaining that Roland is too hotheaded and wild and that he fears the proud hero will "slip up." Thus, Olivier is introduced on the scene of action

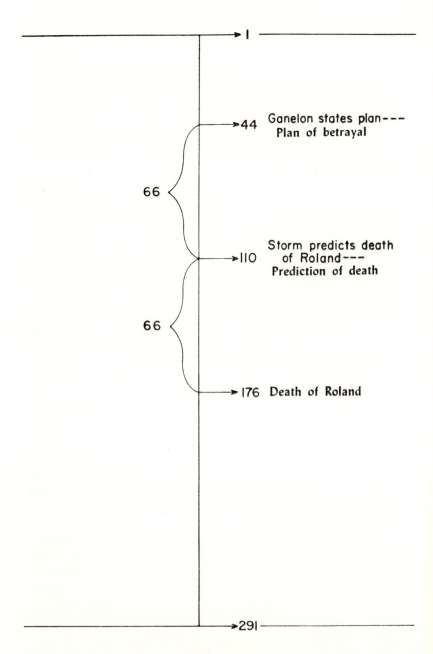

Fig. 1. The Roland theme: Betrayal.

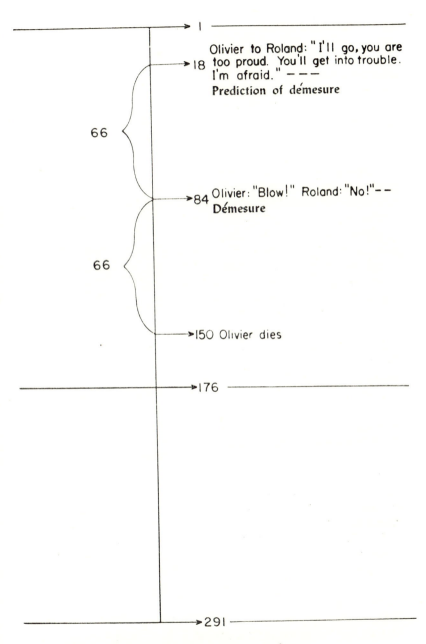

Fig. 2. The Olivier theme: *Démesure.*

uttering a characterization of Roland and bearing a warning of his *démesure*. The set of points established here marks off Olivier's participation in the *démesure* motif: his warning or Prediction of *Démesure* at 18, the action *Démesure* itself at 84, and the Death of Olivier as the result of this action at laisse 150. (See figure 2.)

It now becomes apparent that brackets of 66 laisses from the deaths of the two heroes do in fact touch on such important points in the narrative that the likelihood that they were intended as structural units may be deemed considerable. If such is indeed the case, then it might be expected that a significant event would occur at point 66. This laisse, the first which begins *"Halt sunt li pui . . . ,"* marks a transition in the action. Roland has just completed the disposition of his commands by naming Gualter de l'Hum to hold the narrow defile. Now the final separation occurs, as the main body of Charlemagne's army sets out for France. Charles is in anguish on leaving his nephew behind and seems to be realizing the full import of the tragic mistake of the council in which Ganelon named Roland to command the rearguard.

Sixty-six laisses further on, at laisse 132, the Archbishop Turpin intervenes in the dispute between Roland and Olivier over the blowing of the horn. Proud Roland had refused to blow it when the pagans were first sighted. Now, when he wishes to do so, it is too late. Only 60 of the 20,000 men remain and Olivier has reproached his companion bitterly for his foolhardy bravery. Turpin advises that the horn be blown anyway, for, although it cannot save them, at least Charles will return to avenge their defeat and to bury them.

In effect, the narrative material of laisses 66 and 132 would seem to treat Charlemagne's relation to the tragedy, which, up to this point, might be termed participation by noninvolvement. Nevertheless, the very nonparticipation of Charles was a salient factor in the defeat, and the set of points might be designated: Absence and Anguish of Charles at 66 and the Prediction of his Return for Vengeance and Burial at 132. (See figure 3.)

From the pattern of the two sets of three points previously

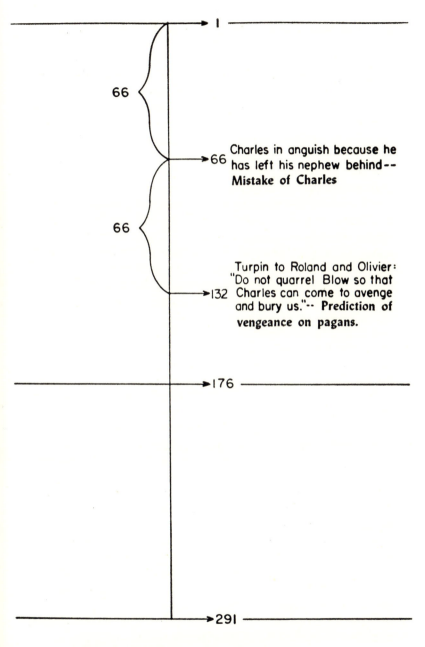

Fig. 3. The Charlemagne theme: Absence.

described, one would also expect in the third set a third point which would treat some aspect of Charlemagne's return for vengeance or burial, but laisse 198 on which it would fall tells of Marsile's request for aid from Baligant, and has no narrative connection with the theme of Charlemagne's relation to the defeat. The reason for this puzzling but significant irregularity will later become apparent.

In general, patterns based on the number 66 cannot be carried out further in the poem as it now stands, for extensions of 66 brackets to any point below that of Roland's death do not coincide with related narrative material. It is to be inferred, therefore, that, in the Oxford version of the epic, the 66 pattern ends with the death of Roland. Figure 4 shows the interlocking pattern of the three narrative sets treating the factors of the tragedy: the *Démesure* set, the Betrayel set, and the King's set. It is rather startling that the numbers of the laisses at each narrative point (i.e., 18, 44, 66, 84, 110, 132, 150, and 176) are all divisible, either by eleven, or by six, or by eleven and six. Naturally, the intervals between the narrative points established by the 66 brackets form a regular pattern. Thus, as can be seen in figure 5, they run 18:26:22; 18:26:22; 18:26:22; and it is interesting that, when viewed in another way as 44:22:44:22:44, the series comprises numerals which are also divisible by eleven.

The regularity of these patterns would seem to substantiate the tentative postulation that there was intent to use as a structural unit in an arithmetic scheme the interval of 66 laisses between the prediction of Roland's death and the death itself. Especially significant is the fact that the narrative points are all divisible by either 11 or 6 or both, for it will be recalled that the laisses chosen to initiate at least two of the three sets of points were selected for *their narrative importance alone* (i.e., the deaths of the two heroes, Roland and Olivier) and not for any numerical relation between them. It appears then, that the probability is considerably beyond chance that the poet wished to construct an arithmetic pattern based on brackets of 66 laisses arranged on narrative points which mark off the basic themes of the tragedy.

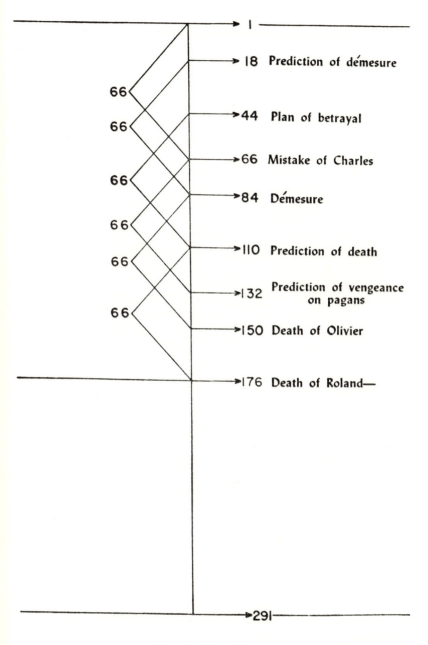

Fig. 4. The 66 pattern.

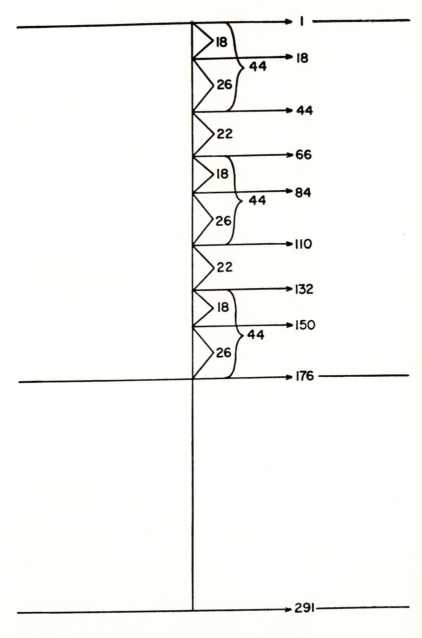

Fig. 5. The 66 pattern (reverse).

A Symbolic Interpretation of the 66 Pattern

If it can now be said with some certainty that an arithmetic structure was intended in the Oxford *Roland*, the next question to be answered is: in what way is the structure metaphoric? The outstanding numbers of the pattern appear to be 66, 11, and 6. In terms of the arithmetic reasoning of the Middle Ages, where, as has been shown in chapter 1, the allegorical meaning or *sensus* of numbers was conceived as an intrinsic component of their natures, these three numbers would be considered inextricably interrelated, for the number 66 is not only the aggregate of 11 (that is, the sum of all the numbers from 1 to 11 equals 66), but it is the product of 11 when multiplied by 6; and it would be further significant in medieval reasoning that the number 66 is composed of two sixes.

From Pythagorean times, the number six was considered extraordinary by reason of its being the first "perfect" number, since it equals the sum of one, two, and three, its aliquot parts or divisors exclusive of itself.[14] Beginning with Philo Judaeus, the mathematical perfection of the number 6 came to be interpreted in biblical exegesis as an allegorical statement and supporting argument for the perfection of God's creation, which was accomplished in six days.[15] Following in this tradition Saint Augustine reasons that the perfection of God's work is signified by 6 because "the number 6 is the *first* which is made up of its own parts, i.e., of its sixth, third, and half, which are respectively 1, 2, and 3, and which make a total of 6."[16] Dante interprets the sixth heaven as the age of earthly perfection, and calls it the mirror of divine justice (*Paradiso XIX*).

But consistency was not an attribute of the symbolic interpretation of numbers, and the perfection of 6 was overlooked when, in the Alexandrian period, as the product of 2, the first "feminine" number, and of 3, the first "masculine" number, it was quite generally held to be the female marriage number by the Neo-Pythagoreans.[17] Things went from bad to worse with 6 when, in Christian times, it was called the number of Venus by Capella (*De nuptiis* 7), and, with the help of homonymous confusion of the Latin *sex, seni* 'six' and *sexus, sexūs* 'sex,' it came to signify the *officia naturalia* of original sin.[18] Doubtless this quality of the number six lead John the Divine to choose it as the component of the number 666, which he assigns to the beast in the Book of Revelation.[19]

The number eleven had been characterized by the Pythagoreans as a "transgression outside of measure," since it exceeds by one the number ten, which was conceived as an aspect of the highly regarded unity.[20] In Christian allegory, eleven was called the number of excess because it exceeded ten, which had come to symbolize the law of the Ten Commandments. Thus, Saint Augustine interprets the number eleven as a "going beyond" or transgression of the law, and therefore, sin.[21] It is perhaps also significant that, of the ten ditches of the inferno, Dante describes the ninth as twenty-two miles in circumference, and the last, reserved for the counterfeiters, as 11 miles (*Inferno XXIX, XXX*). Thus Dante progressively decreases the circumference of the pit by a unit of eleven, which, no doubt following the tradition of Augustine, he took for a number signifying transgression and sin.

It is unfortunate that the poet of the Roland does not tell us, as Dante so often did, what reasoning he followed in his application of number symbolism. In the absence of precise indications of such intent, we can only resort to a rather speculative application of the evidence we have relating to the traditional manner of interpreting numbers. Thus, given the arithmetic pattern and some knowledge of the kind of symbolic manipulations which were available as models, an approximation of the allegorical meaning might be stated as follows: Of the three numbers, 66, 11, and 6, which appear to be outstanding in the numerical structure, the number 11 was probably considered dominant, since from 11 can be generated its aggregate 66. The signification "excess" or "transgression of measure" by which the number 11 was characterized immediately suggests, of course, the sin of *démesure*, Roland's excessive fortitude and a major factor of his downfall, while the number 66, when taken in the sense of the pejorative aspects of its component 6, could signify some aspect of evil. Thus, it might be reasoned that, just as the number 11 generates as its aggregate the number 66, so the *démesure* of Roland, like a seed of destruction, generates Ganelon's hatred of his stepson. This hatred in turn was made manifest in the betrayal, which, abetted by a further act of *démesure* on the part of Roland in the hornblowing episode, achieved its catastrophic fruition in the debacle of the defeat. Roland, then, was an "eleven," the number of his *démesure*,[22] and it is worthy of note that it is laisse 110 (mystically the equivalent of 11)[23] which predicts his death: the storm and eclipse over France are "the great sorrow for the death of Roland."[24]

It would follow that the number 66, as the culmination of the excess of 11, would symbolize the tragic downfall of Roland, and perhaps also the extermination of the twelve peers and the rearguard. However, when viewed in the light of its similarity to the number 666 of the beast of Revelation, the number 66 would also be appropriate for the traitor Ganelon, a Judas type, who, in his conspiracy with the pagan king, did not perhaps accomplish the threefold degree of evil of *the* Beast, but who certainly could qualify as a minor beast. It is possible too that, aside from being conceived as the aggregate of 11, the number 66 was understood in addition as its product when multiplied by 6. Viewed in this light, the number 6 could have been taken in its positive aspect of a symbol of the perfection of God's creation manifested in the hero Roland without his flaw, which, when multiplied by the number of excess, attains the negative qualities of 66, the number of evil by reason of the negative aspects of its component 6, and again a symbol of the destruction of Roland.

In summary, the metaphoric significance which is postulated for the arithmetic structure so far revealed is as follows: Of the three basic numbers, 66, 11, and 6, the dominant number 11, traditionally signifying excess, most certainly symbolizes Roland's *démesure*, while the number 66, as the aggregate of the number of excess, symbolizes the destruction of Roland and the rearguard, and may also, by its association with the number of the beast of Revelations symbolize the traitor Ganelon. Finally, the number 6, as the alternate factor of 66, through its interpretation as the number of the perfection of God's creation, may symbolize the original perfect state of Roland before being brought to ruin through excess.

The 91 Pattern: Arithmetic Structure

The fact that the pattern based on brackets of 66 laisses could not be extended beyond the point of Roland's death in a manner that makes any narrative sense suggests that it was constructed exclusively for the Roncevaux episode. However, when an arc is established between the point of the hero's death in laisse 176 and the point of his burial in laisse 267, a new pattern begins to emerge which embraces the whole of the poem. The bracket between the death and the burial comprises 91 laisses, and, when extended back from the point of death, falls on laisse 85, the third in that series of three exactly similar laisses in which Roland refuses to blow the horn, a narrative point which, in the 66 pattern, was designated the action *Démesure*.[25] The points thus established would tell the story: *Démesure* at 85, Death of Roland at 176, and Burial at 267. (See figure 6.)

Since two of the points of the new set of brackets coincide with points already established in the 66 pattern, it would seem logical to try other laisses in the 66 pattern as generating points for sets of brackets in 91 laisses. Laisses 18 and 44, the points previously designated Prediction of *Démesure* and Plan of Betrayal, are productive. Thus, starting from laisse 18, and arcing forward by 91 laisses to 109, and thence to 200, a point 91 laisses from the end at 291 is attained, and a set is formed which counterpoises that in the 66 pattern starting 66 laisses from the beginning (See figure 7.) Laisse 109 is the first of a series of 3 laisses of transition between the first attack of the Saracens and the second when Marsile arrives with his army. These laisses are full of foreboding and presages of doom (it will be recalled that laisse 110, the central one, foretells the death of

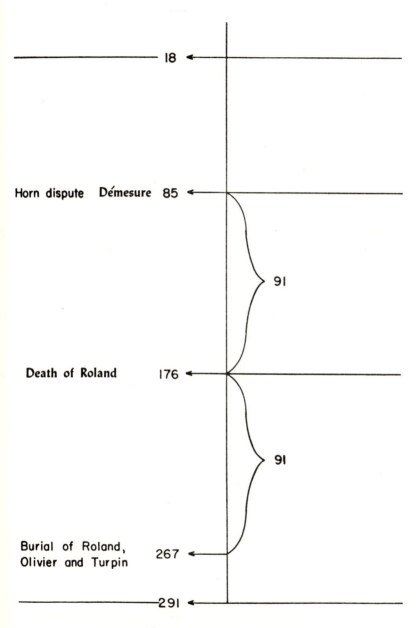

Fig. 6. *Démesure, Death, and Burial.*

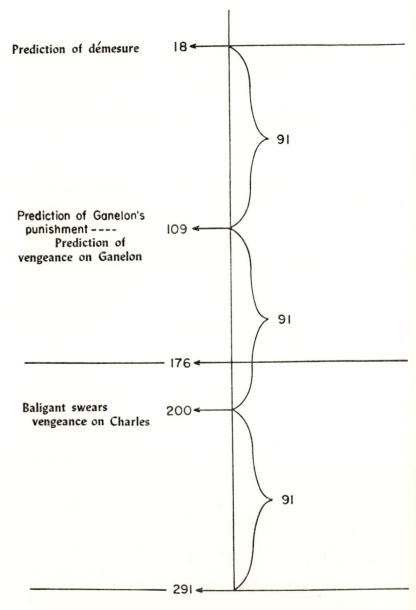

Fig. 7. Predictions: *Démesure*, Vengeance on Ganelon,
Baligant's oath of Vengeance.

Roland). In laisse 109 the jongleur comments on the betrayal of Ganelon and gives his audience advance notice of the trial at Aix, where the condemned traitor will be dismembered and his thirty relatives all hung. In laisse 200, the Saracen emir Baligant, when informed of the losses sustained by King Marsile and of the close proximity of Charlemagne's army, swears to make Charles pay with his head for the right hand that Marsile lost in his battle with Roland. In this set of brackets are interwoven the themes of *Démesure* at 18, Prediction of Vengence on Ganelon at 109, and Baligant's Oath of Vengeance on Charles at 200.

A set of brackets of 91 laisses beginning at laisse 44, where Ganelon reveals his plan of betrayal, would fall on laisses 135 and 226. In laisse 135, Roland blows the horn for the third time and is heard by Charles and the French. Duc Naimes, warning Charles that Roland is in distress, and openly accusing Ganelon of treachery, shakes the emperor from his somewhat somnolent lethargy. The traitor now stands accused by a member of the king's council, and Charles turns back to aid Roland in the following laisse. In laisse 226, Charles, after having disposed his army for the attack on Baligant, prays to God that he may avenge the death of Roland. Now, with clear and assured face he leads off his army while the olifant, sounding above all the other horns, causes the French to weep for pity of Roland. This set of points would seem to relate the narrative: Plan of Betrayal at 44, Traitor Accused to Charles at 135, Charles Prays for Vengeance at 226. (See figure 8.)

The interlocking of the three sets of points of the 91 pattern may be seen in figure 9; and figure 10 shows that, starting from laisse 18, the series of intervals between the narrative points runs: 26:41:24; 26:41:24; 26:41:24. The choice of brackets of 91 laisses would seem to parallel somewhat the arithmetic reasoning which lead to the choice of the number 66, for, just as 66 represents both the aggregate of 11 and its product when multiplied by 6, so 91 represents both the aggregate of 13 (the next prime after 11) and its product when multiplied by 7 (the next integer after 6). However, none of the points established

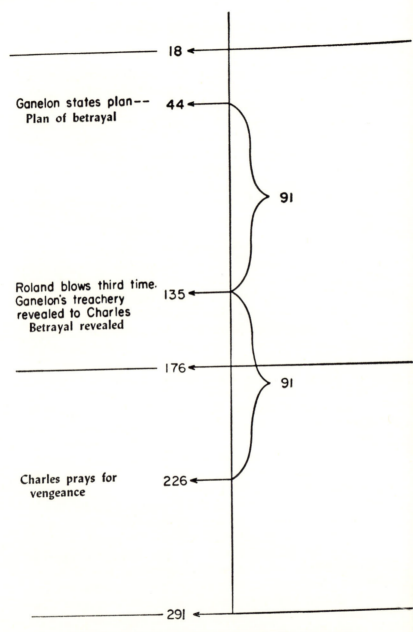

Fig. 8. Betrayal, Betrayal revealed, Charlemagne's
prayer for Vengeance.

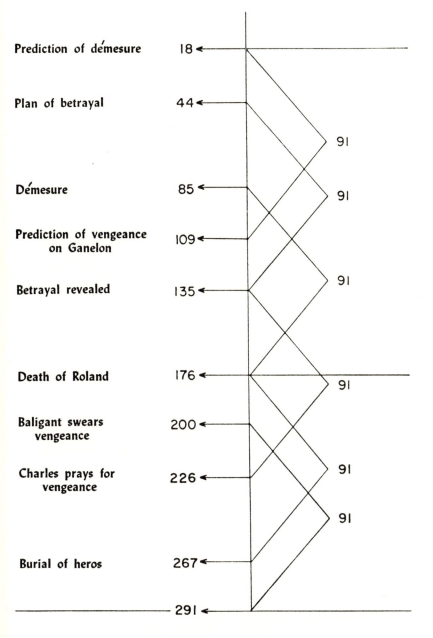

Fig. 9. The 91 pattern.

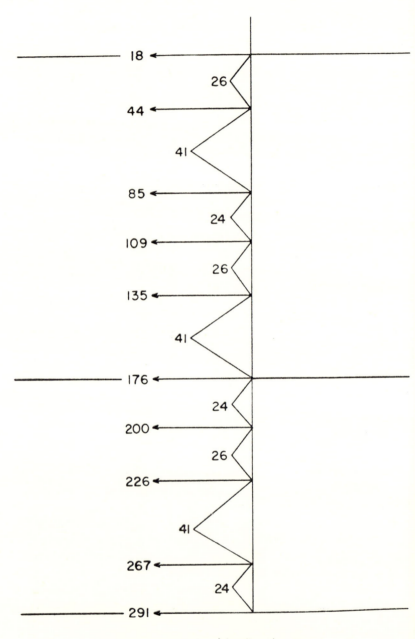

Fig. 10. The 91 pattern (reverse).

for the 91 pattern are divisible, either by 13, or by 7, as was the case with those of the 66 pattern.

Somewhat favoring the probability that a pattern based on brackets of 91 laisses was intended by the poet is the sequence 26:41:24, for, if the two sections of 41 and 24 laisses are grouped together in a larger section of 65 laisses, the sequence of the 91 pattern would be (after 18) 26:65; 26:65; 26:65, the number 26 capable of being expressed as 2 times 13, and the number 65, as 5 times 13 (note that the sum of 2 and 5 equals 7, of necessity the other divisor of 91). This is directly comparable to the 66 pattern, 44:22; 44:22; 44, where the number 44 can be expressed as 4 times 11, and the number 22 as 2 times 11 (note also that the sum of 4 and 2 must equal 6, the alternate divisor of 66).

It will be recalled that the four narrative points of the 66 pattern from which the sets of the 91 pattern are generated are: Prediction of *Démesure* (18), Plan of Betrayal (44), Action of *Démesure* (85), and Death of Roland (176). Thus the upper part of the pattern treats the motifs: betrayal, excess, and death. The remaining five narrative points of the 91 pattern would seem to treat the motifs of vengeance and burial in fulfillment of Turpin's prediction at point 132 of the 66 pattern. Thus, beginning with the Prediction of Vengeance on Ganelon in laisse 109, they run: Traitor Accused to Charles (135), Baligant's Oath of Vengeance on Charles (200), Charlemagne's Prayer for Vengeance (226), and the Burial (267).

That vengeance and burial was indeed the primary theme of the 91 pattern is substantiated by the parallels between the two blocks of 41 laisses shown in figure 11. In the first block between the revelation of Ganelon's betrayal and the death of Roland, the Archbishop Turpin, Olivier, and Roland make their last stand and the final destruction of the rearguard is accomplished. In the second block, between Charlemagne's prayer for vengeance and the burial of the heroes, Charlemagne's battle with Baligant takes place and vengeance on the pagans is done. The diagram shows how, laisse after laisse of destruction *by* the pagans is counterpoised, 91 laisses later, by act after act of vengeance *on* the pagans—vengeance performed under the leadership of a now vital and active Charles, who is alert and keen to get the job done.

The most salient area of correspondence occurs in the two

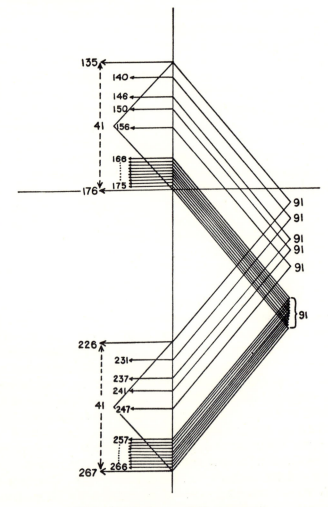

Fig. 11.   Defeat and Vengeance.

groups of 11 laisses from 166 to 176 and 256 to 267 respectively. In laisse 166, the Archbishop Turpin dies; in 257, his pagan counterpart, the Saracen priest Amboire, is killed by Ogier. In the 10 laisses which follow Turpin's death are related the last acts of Roland: the lament for Turpin, the killing of the Saracen with the horn, the attempts to break the sword, the tendering of the glove, the confession of sin, the descent of Gabriel and the other angels, and the death and ascent of the soul in Gabriel's arms. As if in direct answer to this section, 91 laisses further on, the conclusive acts of vengeance on the pagans are performed: Charles engages in personal combat with Baligant, and, with the help of Gabriel, kills the pagan leader. Then the pagans retreat; King Marsile dies of wounds and grief; Charles takes the city of Zaragoza; the pagans are baptized; and finally, in laisse 267, Charles sets out for France, places the horn at Bordeaux, buries the heros at Blaye, and arrives home at Aix for the trial of Ganelon.

A Symbolic Interpretation of the 91 Pattern

It thus becomes apparent that the major function of the 91 pattern was to link the tragedy of Roncevaux, in which Charlemagne's role was one of rather lethargic nonparticipation, with the vigorous and positive acts by Charles to avenge the defeat. It follows that the question next to be answered will be, In what way do the oustanding numbers of the 91 pattern symbolize vengeance? As in the 66 pattern, the basic numbers were 66, 11, and 6, so here the basic numbers would be 91, 13, and 7, of which 13 was no doubt considered dominant by reason of the fact that it produces 91 as its aggregate and at the same time is a factor of 91 when multiplied by 7.

From the paucity of examples of the usage of the number thirteen in Christian allegory offered by Vincent Hopper, it is to be inferred that the church paid little attention to this number beyond explaining the thirteen signs of the cross made for the New Testament at mass as the sum of ten for the law of the

Old Testament and three for the faith in the Trinity of the New.[26] Hopper maintains that the unluckiness of thirteen seems to stem from popular superstition and to be entirely disconnected with the science of numbers as developed in theological tradition (p. 131). It would seem, however, that ecclesiastical reticence regarding the evil connotations of a number which, to every Christian mind, would suggest the thirteen who sat at the table of the Last Supper indicates that the number was in fact either so awful, or so holy, that it was enshrouded in an aura of taboo.[27]

Hopper avers that, in popular superstition, "with every traditional 12, a thirteenth is somehow associated," and he cites Böklen to the effect that the intercalated thirteenth lunar month, of which the raven was the symbol, was regarded as discordant and unlucky.[28] The thirteenth person is treated with a marked degree of ambivalence and is variously interpreted as simply the leader of twelve, or as a leader or hero who must sustain an ordeal, or as the traitor who brings about the downfall of the leader. Thus Hopper notes that the Siege Perilous of the *Livre de Lancelot del Lac* XXXIX, "wherein never knight sat that he met not death thereby," was sanctified but unlucky for the wrong person and, citing Jesse Weston, points to the fact that, in the Modena *Perceval*, the thirteenth chair is in one place reserved for "Nostre Sire" and in another, for the traitor Judas.[29]

Of import to the interpretation of the number thirteen in connection with the *Roland* are some indications within the context of the Charlemagne matter itself regarding the relation between Charles and the twelve peers. In a manuscript belonging to the monastery of San Millán de la Cogolla on the border between Castille and Navarre, there is recorded a short summary of the story of Roland at Roncevaux. The resumé is known as the *Nota Emilianense*, and was written between 1065 and 1075. Here it is stated that, when Charles entered Spain, he had twelve "nephews" (*duodecim neptis*) and that each of them served the king in his entourage for one month (*et unusquisque singulos menses serbiebat ad regem cum scolicis suis*).[30]

According to Menéndez-Pidal, analogy of the group of twelve peers with the twelve apostles is established in the Old-Norse version of the *Roland,* where it is stated that, when Charles started his expedition to Spain, he instituted the twelve peers to combat the pagans "come Dieu a choisi les apôtres pour répandre sa parole sur le monde" (p. 397). Although here, as in the case of the *Nota Emilianense,* the identification of Charles as the thirteenth is not made overtly, the implication is to be inferred.

Finally, however, in that marvelously strange *Pèlerinage de Charlemagne,* the analogy is developed in full. Here, Charlemagne, on arriving in Jerusalem, enters, together with his twelve peers, the chapel of a monastery where the Lord Jesus Christ and the twelve apostles had sung mass. The twelve chairs are still standing in the chapel, with the thirteenth in the center, carefully sealed. The intrepid Charles walks right up and sits down to rest for a while in the thirteenth chair, and the twelve peers take their places on either side of him. While sitting there, so glorious is their appearance that a Jew who happens to be passing through the chapel is converted on the spot and rushes off to tell the Patriarch of Jerusalem: "I saw 12 counts enter that monastery, and with them the thirteenth; never saw I one so handsome. In my opinion, it must be God himself. He and the 12 apostles have come to visit you" (lines 137–40).[31]

The evidence of the *Pèlerinage de Charlemagne* would seem sufficient to substantiate an assumption that the inventor of the 91 pattern, inspired by an association which derived ultimately from the popular imagination, chose the number thirteen as a symbol for Charlemagne. Thus, just as Roland was an "eleven" in the 66 pattern, so Charles is a "thirteen" in the 91 pattern, a "thirteen" who is understood most certainly as the leader of the twelve peers, and no doubt also as the Holy Roman Emperor of the West, who was entitled to occupy the thirteenth chair, the Siege Perilous of the leader of Western Christendom. It is also not unlikely that, in addition, the ecclesiastical interpretation was felt to be conveyed in the number, with the result that Charles was conceived as well in the role of bearer to the pagans of the law of the Old Testament and the faith in the Trinity of the New.

Within the context of the Vengeance theme, it could be reasoned that, as the aggregate of 13, the number of the Christian leader and bearer of the law, the number 91 would symbolize the vengeance and Christian triumph accomplished by the leader in the final defeat and baptism of the pagans. The only interpretation of this number known to the writer is that of a reference by Hopper to the effect that, by gematriatic reasoning, the number 91 was equated with both "Amen" and "Jahveh Adonai" in the Hebrew cabals (pp. 63, 64). The probability that such might also have been the understanding of the poet who worked out the 91 pattern is somewhat heightened by the fact that his choice of the number thirteen as the number of Charles was determined mainly by an extra-ecclesiastical interpretation rooted in popular superstition. In any event, the cabalistic understanding of the number 91 would accord rather well with the concept of the conclusive acts of the avenging Charles, as the earthly representative of Jehovah, the avenging God of the Old Testament.

The number seven has been so charged with symbolic meaning throughout the ages of recorded history that it is difficult to hazard a guess as to which traditional *sensus* a medieval poet would attribute to it. From the time of the earliest astronomical observations of the Babylonians and Chaldeans, as the number of days of duration of each of the four phases of the lunar cycle, as the number of the observable stars in the constellations Pleïades and Bear, as the number of planets known to the ancient world, the number seven has been a sign of both baleful import and sacred significance. By medieval times, the ubiquitous number seven could signify—to enumerate but a few of its qualities—the seven days of creation, the seven gifts of the Holy Spirit, the seven petitions of the Lord's prayer, the seven virtues, the seven deadly sins, the seven beatitudes, the seven liberal arts, the seven steps of wisdom, the seven dolors of the Virgin, the seven tones of the musical scale.[32]

An interpretation of this number which was no doubt widely known can be traced to Saint Augustine, who calls the number seven the symbol of all numbers and equates it with perfect completeness. Augustine reasons further that, since, in the number seven, as the sum of three and four, are combined the spiritual qualities of the Triune Godhead and the temporal qualities of the four-squareness of earth, the number represents the sum of the world-soul and the world, and the soul and body of man, and is, therefore, the number of the universe and of man signifying creation, and the creature as opposed to the Creator.[33]

In view of the Augustinian interpretation, it could be reasoned that the signification of the number 7, as the factor of 91 when multiplied by 13, parallels that of the number 6, as the factor of 66 when multiplied by 11. Thus, just as, in its beneficent aspect, the number 6 signified the perfection of God's creation manifested in Roland the hero, so the number 7 would be equated with the completeness of Charles the creature as opposed to the Creator. And it would follow that, just as the "sixness" of Roland, when multiplied by 11, the number of his *démesure*, produced the baleful 66, so the "sevenness" of Charles, when multiplied by 13, the number of his election as the leader of Christendom and bearer of the law and the faith, produces the conclusive vengeance implied in 91.

In summary, then, of the outstanding numbers, 91, 13, and 7, the dominant number 13 would most certainly signify Charlemagne, the leader of Christendom, while the number 7 would symbolize the completeness of Charles the creature, the earthly representative of his Creator. Finally, the number 91, as the aggregate of 13 and its product when multiplied by 7, would, from the implications of the context, signify the acts of vengeance and Christian justice accomplished by Charles, and may possibly bear connotations of the finality of the acts of Jahveh Adonai, the avenging God of the Old Testament and the law.

---

1. Gaston Paris, ed. (*La Vie de Saint Alexis, poème du XIe siècle et renouvellements des XIIe, XIIIe et XIVe siècles avec préfaces, variantes, notes et glossaire*, pp. 43–45) cites Mabillon, *Acta Ordinis S. Benedicti*, saec. III, pp. 378–79: "Ille Tetbaldus Vernonensis, qui multorum gesta sanctorum, sed et sancti Wandregisili, a sua latinitate transtulit atque in communis

linguae usum satis facunde refudit, ac sic ad quamdam tinnuli rhythmi similitudinem urbanas ex illis cantilenas edidit." Paris translates the Latin passage: "Ce Tedbalt de Vernon qui a traduit de leur latinité les vies de plusieurs saints et entre autres celle de saint Wandrille, les a refondues pour l'usage de la langue commune avec assez d'éloquence, et en a fait d'agréables chansons d'après une sorte de rhythme tintant."

2. Ramón Menéndez-Pidal, *Poesía juglaresca y orígenes de las literaturas románicas*, pp. 38, 39: "Los moralistas del siglo XIII separan como únicos juglares dignos aquellos que se dedican a cantar las gestas de los príncipes y las vidas de los santos." See also p. 291: "Un moralista inglés de entonces reconocía como únicos juglares no pecaminosos a los . . . 'qui cantant gesta principium et vitas sanctorum.'"

3. Joseph Bédier, *Les légendes épiques*, 3:367 ff.

4. Ramón Menéndez-Pidal (*La Chanson de Roland et la tradition épique des Francs*) gives a complete summary and critical evaluation of the history of *Roland* scholarship until 1960.

5. See the reevaluation of the Arabic and Latin documents by Menéndez-Pidal (*La Chanson*, pp. 263–336, 519–32): Mention of the defeat at Roncevaux does not occur in the royal annals until after the year 829 (pp. 276–79), and the name Hruodlandus first appears as that of a participant of the battle of Roncevaux in the *A*-group manuscripts of Eginhard's *Vita Karoli Magni Imperatoris*, written between 828 and 836 (pp. 279–91). Menéndez-Pidal reasons that the late mention of the name argues for the existence of contemporaneous legendary accounts of Roland's exploits.

6. Menéndez-Pidal (*La Chanson*, p. 34) summarizes and provides a bibliography of the findings of Henri Grégoire which suggest that some of the events of the Baligant episode reflect Guiscard's expedition.

7. Jules Horrent (*La Chanson de Roland dans les littératures française et espagnole au moyen âge*, pp. 292–97), taking into account the earliest record known to him at the time of writing of a pair of brothers or relatives named Roland and Olivier, proposes that an arrangement of the Roncevaux episode which includes all the matter of the Oxford version except the Baligant episode was made between the last years of the tenth century and circa 1050. Horrent maintains further that this early version of the *Chanson de Roland* was composed in written form from preexisting material by a true artist and that the poet was a cleric of northern France (pp. 306, 307).

Martin de Riquer (*Los Cantares de gesta franceses*, pp. 120–25), basing his argument on the identification of Turoldus as a Norman monk in the service of William the Conqueror, one Turoldus de Fécamp (d. 1098) abbot of Malmsbury and Peterborough, dates before 1098 the composition of the version of Digby-23 incorporating the Baligant story. He establishes the *terminum ante quem* by the mention in the text of drums and camels, which were introduced into Spain by the Almorávides in 1086. See also Ettori Li Gotti, *La Chanson de Roland e i Normanni*. The date proposed by Riquer accords well with that established by Grégoire. (See note 6, above.) A critical survey of opinions on the inclusion of the Baligant episode is given by Menéndez-Pidal (*La Chanson*, pp. 121–29).

8. For *L*, the most complete manuscript of the *Alexis*, see *La Vie de Saint Alexis*, ed C. Storey, p. x. Samaran (*La Chanson de Roland: Réproduction phototypique du manuscrit Digby-23*, p. 30) dates Digby-23 ca. 1125–50.

9. Menéndez-Pidal (*La Chanson*, pp. 470–75), in discussing the relations between the art of the jongleur and that of the clergy, remarks that certain modern critics, in trying to imagine what the *Roland* was like before the Oxford version, have used the *Vie de Saint Alexis* as a point of comparison. He summarizes their opinion concerning this pre-Oxford *Roland*, which they consider "était une histoire de martyrs, exprimant le conflit de la 'prouesse' et de la 'sagesse' dans la lutte contre les Païens: l'oeuvre était écrite, ajoutent-ils, dans le style sévère et la rigoureuse forme strophique du Saint Alexis." See Jules Horrent, *La Chanson de Roland*, p. 302; S. Pellegrini, *La Canzone di Rolando*, pp. 13–14; Maurice Delbouille, *Sur la genèse de la Chanson de Roland*, pp. 163–64; Pierre Le Gentil, *La Chanson de Roland*, p. 86. Menéndez-Pidal disagrees with this position, which posits a regular line and strophic form similar to that of the *Alexis*, on the ground that regularity of line or laisse would have been unlikely for jongleuresque poetry at such an early period.

10. *Les textes de la Chanson de Roland*, Vol. 1.

11. Eleanor Webster Bulatkin, "The Arithmetic Structure of the Old-French *Vie de Saint Alexis*," *PMLA* 74 (1959): p. 495, n. 6. In manuscript *L* of the *Alexis*, five lines are missing, each from a different stanza, but the regularity of the stanzas is proof that they once existed. Obviously, the chance of scribal error increases markedly when, as in the case of the epic laisse, stanzaic division follows no regular pattern.

12. Ernst Robert Curtius (*European Literature and the Latin Middle Ages*, p. 501), cites the *Alexis*, the *Vita Leudegariae*, and the *Carmen de sancto Landberto* as works which manifest structural division at the point of the saint's death, but in his analysis of the structure of the *Alexis* in the article "Zur Interpretation des Alexiusliedes," *ZRPH* 56 (1936): 113–37, he makes no special usage of the point as the basis for an arithmetic pattern.

13. The pertinent lines of the laisses on which narrative points are established are given in table 1 of the appendix.

14. Vincent Foster Hopper, *Medieval Number Symbolism*, p. 40.

15. *The Allegorical Interpretation of Genesis II, III*, book 1, 2, in Philo with an English Translation, by F. H. Colson and G. H. Whitaker, 1:249: "When, then, Moses says, 'He finished His work on the sixth day,' we must understand him to be adducing not a quantity of days, but a perfect number, namely six, since it is the first that is equal to the sum of its own fractions 1/2, 1/3, and 1/6, and is produced by the multiplication of two unequal

factors, 2 x 3: and see, the numbers 2 and 3 have left behind the incorporeal character that belongs to 1, 2 being an image of matter, and being parted and divided as that is, while 3 is the image of a solid body, for the solid is patient of a threefold division."

16. *The City of God*, 11:375.

17. The Greeks, who viewed divisibility as a defect and a falling away from unity, preferred odd numbers and assigned masculine, and therefore good, qualities to them. Even numbers, always divisible, were considered less good and feminine. Thus the odd number five, as the *sum* of the first masculine number three and the first feminine two, was the symbol of marriage in its positive aspects, while the even number six, as the *product* of two times three, was the female symbol of marriage and represented its more negative side. So Plutarch (*Sur l 'E de Delphes*, 8:44–46), with reference to a possible interpretation of the mysterious letter E on the temple of Apollo at Delphi, reasons as follows regarding the number five: 'On l'appelle le nombre 'nuptial,' en raison de l'analogue du nombre pair avec le sexe féminin et du nombre impair avec le sexe masculin. En effet, lorsque on divise les nombres en deux parties égales, le nombre pair se partage entièrement, ne laissant pour ainsi dire à l'intérieur de lui même qu'un espace vide, qui attend d'être comblé, tandis que, si le nombre impair subit la même operation, il y a toujours un reste au milieu après division. Et c'est pourquoi l'impair est plus générateur que l'autre: lorsqu'il lui est uni, il prévaut constamment et n'est jamais dominé, car l'union des deux ne produit jamais un nombre pair, mais toujours un nombre impair. Bien plus, c'est lorsque les nombres de chaque genre—pair et impair—s'adjoignent et s'ajoutent entre eux que la différence devient la plus sensible: aucun nombre pair se combinant avec un autre pair ne peut produire un impair, ni sortir des limites de sa propre nature; faible, et imparfait, le nombre pair est incapable d'engendrer un nombre différent de lui-même. Par contre, les nombres impairs, en s'unissant à d'autres impairs, produisent en foule des nombres pairs, parce que leur vertu génératrice s'exerce en toute circonstance."

18. Cf. the citation of Curtius (*European Literature*, p. 504), from an anonymous Carolingian poem.

19. It is to be noted that, in the symbolic interpretation of numbers during the Middle Ages, the meaning could remain constant for any decimal position. Thus Hopper remarks that, in his solution of the number 666 of the beast in Revelation, Thomas Acquinas "discusses 6 in relation to unity, 6 in relation to the denarius, and 6 in relation to the hundred. The meaning of 6 itself does not change by reason of its decimal position" (pp. 9, 10).

20. For the Pythagorean interpretation of the number eleven, cf. Hopper, p. 101. In so far as the equation of the number ten with unity, cf. note 19 supra, on the interpretation of decimal positions, and also Hopper, pp. 44 and 45: "Ten and 1 are mystically the same, as are also 100 and 1,000, the 'boundaries' of number."

21. *The City of God*, 15:508: "But in whatever manner the generations of Cain's line are traced downwards, whether it be by first-born sons or by the heirs to the throne, it seems to me that I must by no means omit to notice that, when Lamech had been set down as the seventh from Adam, there were named, in addition, as many of his children as made up this number to *eleven*, which is the number signifying sin; for 3 sons and one daughter were added. . . . Since, then, the law is symbolized by the number 10—whence that memorable Decalogue—there is no doubt that the number 11, which goes beyond 10, symbolizes the transgression of the law, and consequently sin. . . . The progeny of Adam, then, by Cain the murderer, is completed in the number 11, which symbolizes sin; and this number itself is made up by a woman, as it was by the same sex that, in the beginning, was made of sin by which we all die."

22. Cf., for example, the *Vita Nuova* 29, where Beatrice is explained as a "nine," the number of miracle because three, the square root of nine and its unique factor, is the "Factor" of the Holy Trinity.

23. See note 19, supra, on the interpretation of decimal positions.

24. Line 1437: *Co est li granz dulors por la mort de Rollant.*

25. The so-called "parallel laisses," for which the Roncevaux episode of the Oxford *Roland* is noted, are held to be characteristic of epic poetry and no doubt originated as a functional outgrowth of oral transmission. Thus, a jongleur, having at his command more than one version of a given episode, might recite two laisses relating exactly the same narrative events but having different assonance. This was probably done for several reasons: in less artistic renditions, perhaps simply from ignorance and the desire on the part of the jongleur to "tell all he knew," but also for the practical purpose of relaxing the progress of the narrative so that even the most inattentive member of the listening audience would not miss important points of the story. The more talented jongleurs no doubt used them also as an exhibition of their virtuosity in making variations on a theme. In the *Chanson de Roland*, they are used with great artistic effect and at times attain the level of lyric interludes, serving now as a pause between actions to intercalate jongleur's comment and premonitory dreams and visions (cf., laisses 66–68, 109–11, 125, 126), now as a means of emphasizing the high points of the narrative, as in the case of the plan of Ganelon (43–45), the horn dispute (83–85), the blowing of the horn (133–35), and breaking of the sword (171–73), and the lament of Charles for Roland (206–10). They are also used to enumerate long chains of similar events, such as the killing of the pagans by the Christian peers (96–103) or the killing of the Christian peers by the pagans (116–21), or for the repeated actions of battle preparations such as the oaths of the pagans to kill Roland (71–78) or the organization of the ten battle corps of Charles (218–25). Naturally, the device permits flexibility in the arrangement of the narrative and when used in conjunction with a number pattern, provides exactly the quantity of "stuffing" necessary

to make the pattern fit. Therefore, although in the 66 pattern the narrative point *Démesure* fell on laisse 84, since this laisse stands in the center of a group of three which treat identical material, laisse 85 can serve just as well for the same narrative point. The distribution of the parallel laisses in the Oxford *Roland* is shown in figure 16, where the shaded blocks to the left indicate the parallel groups on which points in the number patterns fall.

26. The only other mention made by Hopper of an ecclesiastical interpretation of the number thirteen to which the poet of the *Roland* would have had access refers to the association of this number with the Epiphany, because the three Magi came to visit the infant Jesus when he was thirteen days old (p. 131 n.).

27. It is to be noted that Saint Augustine, *The City of God*, 15:508, in the passage immediately following his disquisition on the number eleven, avoids specific mention of the number thirteen, but implies that the thirteenth person was evil: "But from Adam to Noah in the line of Seth there are 10 generations. And to Noah 3 sons are added, of whom, while one fell into sin, 2 were blessed by their father; so that, if you deduct the reprobate and add the gracious sons to the number you get 12—a number signalized in the case of the patriarchs and of the apostles, and made up of the parts of the number seven multiplied into one another—for 3 times 4 or 4 times 3 give 12."

28. Ernst Böklen, *Die Unglückszal Dreizehn und ihre mythische Bedeutung*, pp. 8, 9.

29. Jesse L. Weston, *The Legend of Sir Perceval*, 2:132.

30. See Menéndez-Pidal (pp. 384–447) for a critical evaluation of the scholarship and implications of the *Nota Emilianense*, the text of which he gives on page 390. He demonstrates that the usage of the term *neptis* 'nephews' derives from a misinterpretation as the Spanish word *primo* 'cousin,' of a hypothetical French or Provençal term *primes,* derived from the *primus in curia*, an alternate designation for the Carolingian *paladin* (p. 396).

31. *Karls des Grossen Reise nach Jerusalem und Constantinople*, p. 9.

32. See Hopper, passim. Cf. Philo, *Allegorical Interpretation*, p. 151 (1:4): "Nature takes delight in the number seven. Thus there are seven planets, the counterpoise to the uniform movement of the fixed stars. It is in seven stars that the bear reaches completeness, and gives rise not to commerce only but to fellowship and unity among men. The changes of the moon, again, occur by sevens: this is the luminary most sympathetic to earthly matters. And such changes as nature produces in the atmosphere, she effects mainly by the influence of figures dominated by seven. Indeed, all that concerns us mortals has a divine origin drawn from heaven and is for our weal when its movement is ruled by seven. Who does not know that seven months' infants come to birth, while those that have taken a longer time, remaining in the womb eight months, are as a rule still-born? And they say a man becomes a reasoning being during his first seven years, . . . and that during his second period of seven years he reaches complete

consummation . . . for at about the age of fourteen we are able to beget offspring like ourselves. The third period of seven years, again, is the end of growth . . . Furthermore the unreasoning side of the soul consists of seven parts, five senses, and the organ of speech, and the genital organ. The body again has seven movements, six mechanical, the seventh circular. Seven also are the internal organs, stomach, heart, spleen, liver, lung, two kidneys. Of equal number in like number are the divisions of the body—head, neck, breast, hands, belly, abdomen, feet. And the face . . . is pierced by seven apertures, by two eyes, and two ears, as many nostrils and the mouth, which make up seven. The excrements are seven—tears, mucus, spittle, seed, super-fluities discharged by two ducts, and the sweat that oozes from all over the body. Once again, in diseases the seventh is the most critical day. And the monthly purgings of women extend to seven days.

The power of this number reaches also to the most beneficent of the arts: in grammar, for instance, the best and most effective of the letters, namely the vowels, are seven in number; in music we may fairly call the seven-stringed lyre the best of instruments, because the enharmonic genus, which as we know is the most dignified of those used in melodies is best brought out when that instrument renders it. Sevenfold are the modulations in pronunciation—acute, grave, circumflex, aspirated and unaspirated, long, short. Further, seven is the first number after the perfect number six, and the same in some sort with the number one."

33. See note 27, supra; and Hopper, p. 84. Cf. Saint Augustine, (*Commentary on the Lord's Sermon on the Mount with Seventeen Related Sermons*, 2:144–46 [II, 10, 36]), who interprets the first three of the seven petitions of the Lord's Prayer as pertaining to the eternal spiritual world to come and the latter four to the needs of temporal life. In *Letter LV*, xv, 28 (*The Confessions and Letters of St. Augustine, with a Sketch of his Life and Work*, 1:312, 313), Augustine remarks: "I regard the number 40 as a fit symbol for this life, because in it the creature (of which the symbolical number is 7) cleaves to the Creator, in whom is revealed that unity of the Trinity which is to be published while time lasts throughout this whole world—a world swept by 4 winds, constituted of 4 elements, and experiencing the changes of 4 seasons of the year." Cf. also *The City of God*, 11:375, 376, with reference to the symbolic completeness of the number 7: "It is often put for all numbers together, as, 'A just man falleth seven times, and riseth up again'—that is, let him fall never so often, he will not perish . . . And many such instances are found in the divine authorities, in which the number 7 is, as I said, commonly used to express the whole, or the completeness of anything. And so the Holy Spirit, of whom the Lord says 'He will teach you the truth,' is signified by this number (Isaiah 11:2, Revelation 3:1). In it is the rest of God, the rest His people find in Him. For rest is in the whole, i.e., in perfect completeness, while in the part there is labour."

The Creation
of the Numerical Patterns

Chapter Three

WHEN THE MAJOR THEMES of the 66 pattern are compared with those of the 91, it becomes evident that while it is Roland who is the protagonist of the 66 pattern by his identification with the dominant number 11, it is Charlemagne, by his identification with the dominant 13, who is the protagonist of the 91 pattern. Thus, to borrow terms which Menéndez-Pidal has borrowed in turn from Pauphilet, in the story of Roncevaux of the 66 pattern we have the *Chanson de Roland,* perhaps that very *Cantilena Rollandi* which William of Malmsbury tells us was sung at the battle of Hastings, while the story of the 91 pattern would be more accurately entitled the *Chanson de Charlemagne.*[1]

From the foregoing interpretations of the significance of the numbers 11 and 13 in the poem's context, it can also be said that the dominant motif of the 66 pattern is *Démesure* and that of the 91 pattern Vengeance. When some of the narrative points on which these patterns are developed are examined in the light of what is now generally held to be the provenience of the Oxford *Roland,* it becomes evident that the motifs manifest origins in cultural milieux which are chronologically quite distinct, and that the 66 pattern may have been in existence as early as the beginning of the eleventh century.

The Problem of Olivier

The theme of Roland's *démesure,* stated in terms of narrative points treating Olivier's death, the horn dispute, and Olivier's initial characterization of Roland as a man of valor lacking prudence, obviously depends for its development upon the inclusion of Olivier in the story. This character, who bears the only name of Latin origin in all the *Roland* matter, and whose identification as the son of a certain *"duc Reiner"* who holds the marches of the "val de Runers" (lines 2208-9) cannot be verified historically or geographically, is generally conceded to be a poetic invention. In 1943 Leo Spitzer demonstrated that the name Olivier, as a derivative of *oliva,* connotes wisdom and peace, as symbolized by the olive tree. From this he infers that the creation of the character Olivier was an exclusively learned innovation which sought to allegorize the concept *sapientia* as opposed to the *fortitudo* of the hero Roland.[2]

Menéndez-Pidal agrees in essence with Spitzer's thesis, but favors a derivation of *Olivier* from *oliva* by means of the vulgar suffix *-arius* rather than by the classic *-erius* which Spitzer had proposed, arguing that *-erius* was rare and, in its uncontaminated form, relatively unproductive in Romance (pp. 345–47). The meaning would thus be a function or an attribute of the tree *oliva* such as "a merchant of olives" or "a bearer of a branch or crown of branches of the olive tree." Menéndez-Pidal mentions that Madame Rita Lejeune recalls the existence of a statue of Hercules bearing the inscription: *Hercules invictus cognominatus vulgo Oliverius* (p. 346). In the Latin documents discussed below the forms *Oliverius* and *Olivarius* are both attested.

From the recent investigations of Madame Lejeune, Paul Aebischer, and others, concerning the mention in legal documents of pairs of brothers or relatives named Olivier and Roland, it is to be inferred that the character Olivier was invented at some date prior to any year in the period from 985 to 1015. According to Madame Lejeune, the earliest document signed by persons named Oliverius and Rollandus which is so far known dates between 999 and 1031 and is located in Velay (Haute-Loire).[3] Menéndez-Pidal reasons that, since the signatories would have to be adult, the youngest would have been born at the latest between 985 and 1015, and concludes that a story telling of the *compagnonnage* of Roland and Olivier was, therefore, circulating in Auvergne at the end of the tenth or the beginning of the eleventh centuries (pp. 355, 356). The earliest attestation found so far of the single name Olivarius was observed by Pio Rajna in a document dated circa 1000 of the *Cartulaire de Savigny* localized at Bribost (Rhone).[4]

Spitzer's explanation of the invention of the name Olivier as the product of a learned ambience is somewhat in conflict with the tendency in neo-traditionalist thought to conceive the origin of the epic in the popular, oral tradition of the jongleurs. Nevertheless, some noted scholars of the modern school have accepted his proposal, reasoning that the Oxford version of the *Roland* in its form and artistry is simply exceptional and that during the eleventh century there must have been circulating a work of genius manifesting clerical influence whose popularity is witnessed by the prevalence, both inside and outside of France, of Roland-Olivier pairs who would have been born during that period.[5]

However, in an extensive series of studies, the celebrated Swiss scholar, Paul Aebischer,[6] rejects in toto Leo Spitzer's interpretation of the name of Olivier and remarks that Spitzer's article, "étant donnée la notoriété de son auteur, exerce sa pernicieuse influence encore aujourd'hui" (p. 167). Paul Aebischer's position in this matter will be examined closely.

Aebischer expresses concern over the relative position of the names Olivier and Roland in the seventeen attestations of the pair of names which have been discovered in legal documents ranging from circa 999–1031 through 1183 (p. 155). In the six attestations up through 1115 which can be certainly dated, the names occur in the order Olivier and Roland; whereas, in the period 1123 to 1183, eight occur in the order Roland and Olivier and only two in the order Olivier and Roland. (An additional attestation in the order Roland and Olivier has been omitted from this count because of uncertainty regarding the date, although the probability is high that it could be assigned to the eleventh century rather than the twelfth.)[7] This ordering of

059663

names has led Aebischer to infer that, during the eleventh century, stories about Olivier and Roland were circulating in which Olivier was characterized as the older of the couple and that parents were inspired by these stories to name the older child Olivier and the younger brother Roland. He reasons further that, conversely, during the twelfth century, the jongleurs must have been reciting a poem in which Roland was the dominant character and Olivier secondary, which inspired parents to name the older child Roland.

To explain this phenomenon, Aebischer advances the theory that the poem of the eleventh century which inspired the Olivier-Roland order was not a pre-Oxford version of the *Chanson de Roland*, but rather a "primitive" version of the epic *Girard de Vienne* of the Guillaume d'Orange cycle. This epic is known to us through the early thirteenth-century poem by Bertran de Bar-sur-Aube[8] and by an early fourteenth-century translation in the *Karlamagnus saga*.[9] Aebischer considers the Norwegian translation "un pâle resumé de la chanson farnçaise" but maintains that it reflects a primitive form of the legend (p. 159).

Aebischer restates points relevant to the topic under discussion in the Norwegian version of the story of the rebellious vassal Girard: The young Roland was armed by his father Milon and presented himself at the camp of his uncle Charlemagne, where he was tutored by four instructors. Girard, the uncle of Olivier, after having been besieged for seven years, resolves to make peace with Charlemagne and sends Olivier with Lambert to sue for the emperor's pardon. The two ambassadors are badly received by Charles, and Olivier is provoked to demand a judicial combat to prove that his uncle Girard is not a traitor. Roland volunteers to champion Charles, and the battle is set to take place outside the walls of Vienne. Lambert and Naimes, to forestall the duel, use their offices to effect a reconciliation between Charles and Girard in which Girard will agree to give fealty for his lands to Charles. The reconciliation is made, and Charles himself disarms the two combatants and enters the city.[10]

Aebischer notes that, in the fourteenth-century manuscript of the *Karlamagnus saga*, a character named *Adeini* is identified as the daughter of *Reinald,* the *jarl* of *Laramel,* and that in another manuscript (of the late seventeenth century) [11] she is called *Audu* and *Audam* and is described as the daughter of *Reinar,* the *jarl* of *Kaliber.* He argues that since Aude is "évidement" the sister of Olivier, the latter is also the son of Reiner, the brother-in-law of Girard.[12]

The facts stated here have persuaded Aebischer to formulate a hypothesis which, in summary, would be as follows: Toward the year 1000 a story was circulating concerning the stand taken at Ronceveaux by Roland, the nephew of Charlemagne. A jongleur engaged in telling of the revolt of the vassal Girard wished to create for Girard a nephew comparable to the nephew of Charles, but since Girard was the protagonist of his story, he wished him to have a nephew who was superior to Charlemagne's and thus made him older and stronger. For this reason, he invented Olivier and his father Reiner (p. 163).

The name which he contrived for his character, maintains Aebischer, was made up after the pattern of other names which he knew like *Christehildis* and *Restemundus,* that is, as a hybrid comprising a Latin base and a Germanic suffix (pp. 167–70). Thus he concocted *Olivier* from the Germanic *-harja.* Aebischer argues that the jongleur wished this name to be like any ordinary proper name and that he did not intend for it to have symbolic overtones (p. 168).

Such a story would thus give parents reason for baptizing the older son Olivier and the cadet Roland. Aebischer implies that, at the beginning of the twelfth century, the poet of the Oxford *Roland* borrowed the character Olivier and his identity as the son of Reiner from the primitive version of the *Girard de Vienne* and that the new characterization of the pair, with Roland now the protagonist, inspired parents to use the name Roland for the older son (p. 163).

In essence the distinguished Swiss scholar offers as evidence in support of his thesis the truncated version of the Norwegian translation which postdates the Oxford *Roland* by 200 years at the earliest and Bertran's *Girard de Vienne* by at least 100 years. Since such evidence could hardly be construed as a concrete proof of anything that was happening in the eleventh century, it becomes apparent that Aebischer's arguments are based entirely on speculation.

Basically Aebischer's thesis can be reduced to two propositions: (1) that the character Olivier was invented for the *Girard de Vienne* matter, and (2) that Olivier was not included in the *Chanson de Roland* matter until the beginning of the twelfth century.

The second proposition is demonstrably disproved by the *Nota Emilianense* of 1065–1075, which names both Roland and Olivier as two of the twelve "nephews" of Charlemagne who were with the king before Zaragoza. Thus this precious text stands as indisputable evidence that a story telling of the Ronceveaux defeat at which Roland was killed was being told at least before 1075, and that in this story Olivier was one of the twelve peers on the expedition to Spain.[13]

However, Aebischer's first proposition must be examined from several points of view, of which perhaps the most important is the development of the two heroes in the *Girard de Vienne* epic. The probability that, during the twelfth century, the jongleurs were reciting stories treating the matter of this epic is not in question. The question is: how did Roland and Olivier get into the stories? And here we have to deal with the problem of the cyclic extension of the biographies of epic heroes, which, as Jean Frappier has so aptly remarked with reference to the Guillaume d'Orange cycle, "a procédé presque regulièrement à rebours de la chronologie."[14] "Les fils ont engendré des pères," he maintains, to which might be added: the heroic death engenders the birth and youth. This phenomenon, so common to all legendary development, is of widespread occurrence in hagiographic material, where, as Hippolyte Delehaye has shown, stories concerning the "life before martyrdom" were created by popular imagination as elaborations of the few sparse facts given in the calendars.[15] That it is met with again in the epic tradition is manifested as well in the vast quantity of *mocedades* material treating the youth of the Cid in the Spanish *romances* as in the various *enfance* epics (*de Vivien, de Garin, de Guillaume*) in the cycle of Guillaume d'Orange. Clearly, the story of the young Roland and his older and wiser companion Olivier in another epic of the Guillaume cycle falls naturally into the normal pattern of cyclic expansion and borrowing. The jongleurs, inspired by the enthusiasm of their audience for the exploits of the two heroes on the field at Ronceveaux, and in response to popular demand, simply invented other stories to explain who the heroes were and how they came to know each other. Perhaps they also invented the character Aude to emphasize further the human reality of the pair. That the poet of the Oxford *Roland* borrowed back from the extended development of the *enfance* stories which could have been circulating in the eleventh century is perfectly possible, and that a popular conception of an Olivier older than Roland could have been derived in part from such stories is also plausible, but that the character Olivier was expressly invented for such an *enfance* is contrary to to the normal progress of legendary evolution.

Given the reverse chronology of the normal cyclic expansion of stories concerning the birth and early years of epic heroes, it is certainly reasonable to suppose that the creation of the character Olivier and the invention of his name had occurred before the composition of the *enfance* material. The normal place to expect the invention would be in the context of the Ronceveaux poem, where the symbolism of the name is inextricably integrated with the role of the character in the central conflict of the poem. A logical explanation for this rather unusual name has been provided by Spitzer. When the logic fits into a broader pattern of logical sequences, why should a construct that works be rejected to favor, as Aebischer would do, an explanation based on fantasy and random choice?

However, the phenomenon which Aebischer originally sought to explain still remains: according to the limited data which we have, the epic material of the eleventh century seems to have inspired parents to name their older sons Olivier and their younger sons Roland, while in the twelfth century the situation was reversed. A partial explanation has been suggested above in the possibility that an *enfance* story could have been a contributing factor in the order of the eleventh century. But the total situation becomes clear only if the possibility of clerical participation in the composition of the *Chanson de Roland* is admitted fully and if the evolving cultural ambience which produced the evolving poem is taken into consideration.

The *Nota Emilianense* gives the names of six of the twelve "nephews" of Charlemagne who were with him before Zaragoza as follows: "Nomina ex his Rodland, Bertland, Oggero Spartacurta, Ghigelmo Alcorbitunas, Olivero et episcopo domini Torpini." Aebischer remarks that, although in this text of 1065–75 the name Roland occurs before that of Olivier, the two names are not contiguous (pp. 170–71). He construes the separation of the names as evidence that the famous *compagnonnage* of the Oxford *Roland* had not been established by this date, and, although elsewhere he takes the position that Olivier was not in the *Chanson de Roland* at all until the Oxford version, he tentatively suggests when discussing the *Nota* that perhaps the mention of Olivier in the eleventh-century text is evidence that the character got into the Roland story in two waves: in the first simply as one of the participating knights; in the second, as the fully developed character of the Oxford version (p. 163).

It is to be noted, however, that Olivier is listed in the *Nota* as the next before the bishop Turpin, a fact which Aebischer has overlooked, and which might indicate, if the ordering of the names has any meaning at all, that Olivier is conceived to participate more in the ambience of the clergy than in that of the other knights.

During the tenth and early eleventh centuries, the clergy, in their efforts to subdue the continual internecine warfare of the period and to bring some order to an age of frightful violence, espoused the cause of the wisdom and prudence of *sapientia* as opposed to the destructive bravery of *fortitudo*.[16] Thus it would be entirely with the limits of historic probability to suppose that Olivier was invented under the inspiration of the clergy as an exemplification of the clerical position and that, since wisdom is the natural concomitant of maturity, this character would have been understood from the moment of its inception as the elder of the pair. No doubt, at the time of baptism the clergy would not have hesitated to explicate the poem to parents who showed inclination to misunderstand its meaning.

However, if the Olivier of the eleventh century was, with the help of the clergy, established in the popular mind as the elder and wiser of the pair, what could have caused the reversal of this understanding in the twelfth century?

Toward the end of the eleventh century the attitude of the church in regard to the effectiveness and desirability of emphasizing *sapientia* as a means of controlling the fratricidal warfare within the confines of Western Christiandom seems to have been shifting to a new position. The fighting energy of the feudal barons was now to be consecrated and directed toward a common enemy in the crusades against the Saracens. Thus when, at the Council of Clermont of November 26, 1095, Urban II made the famous pronouncement: "Let the truce of God be observed at home and let the arms of Christians be directed to winning Jerusalem," ecclesiastical sanction was conferred on the *militiae dei*. Valor as a virtue could take precedence over prudence, since valor was to be directed, not against brothers, but against an enemy outside of the Christian community. The ancient virtues of Charlemagne's time were resurrected, and the spirit of this mighty leader of the Christian world was invoked for guidance in the renewed fight against the pagan. A new version of the old song about Roland was needed, a version which would emphasize the vitality of Charles the Crusader. With a small amount of retouching to change the image of Charles from the portrait of the weak and rather indecisive Carolingian of the end of the dynasty to that of the avenger of Christendom the old song could be made to serve the purpose. (As will later be demonstrated, the reworking was really not very well done.) And so the Oxford *Roland* came into being. Wisdom and prudence were old-fashioned now, and the fortitude of Roland became the new ideal. And no doubt, at the time of baptism the clergy again exercised their ingenuity to explicate the new version.

Thus it would seem that, with the invention of the character Olivier at the beginning of the eleventh century, there was inaugurated a special way of evaluating the deeds of Roland. In his more primitive conception, Roland would have been like all heroes, simply a man evincing bravery and strength in the face of catastrophe, and was not required to manifest perfection or wisdom or moderation.[17] Then, in being counterpoised against Olivier, Roland was made to acquire a defective flaw, by reason of the excess of that very quality which had made him a hero. The invention of the 66 pattern, with arithmetic stress on the concept *excess,* is thus shown to be a device comparable to the choice of the name Olivier for expressing metaphorically the conflict *sapientia versus fortitudo.* Finally, with the Oxford revision, the revitalization of Charlemagne and the revival of emphasis on his crusading mission provided a setting for a reversion to the primitive, pre-Olivier conception of Roland. Thus, although the *sapientia-fortitudo* conflict remained in the work, under the guidance of the clergy, popular understanding of the relations between the heroes placed Roland in the dominant position.

That the arithmetic structure was introduced into the *Roland* material at the same time as the invention of Olivier cannot be stated with certainty, but to assume that it was not necessitates positing the participation of another revisionist equally as learned as the one who conceived Olivier and with the same inclination toward symbolic reasoning. Furthermore, since the inclusion of Olivier required extensive rearrangement of the material, it would be natural to assume that the arithmetic pattern was introduced at the same time. Finally, the probability that the arithmetic structure and the invention of Olivier were coetaneous is somewhat heightened by the chronological implications of another narrative point of the 66 pattern.

France at the End of the Carolingian Dynasty

Menéndez-Pidal discusses the inquiries initiated by Ferdinand

Lot and carried on by Robert Fawtier, Emil Mireaux, and René Louis, which lead to the conclusion that certain laisses retained in the Oxford *Roland* indicate that a revision of the Roland material took place during or shortly after the period between the years 987, when the Carolingian dynasty succumbed to Hugh Capet, and 991, when the last Carolingian, Charles of Lorraine, was captured at Laon (pp. 331–36). These conclusions are deduced from laisses which mention the age of Charlemagne, others which name the capital as Laon, and another which describes the geographical extent of France.

In 1943, Mireaux suggested that the age of 200 years, attributed to Charles by Marsile in laisses 40–42, could represent the two centuries, 768–987, during which the Carolingian dynasty occupied the throne. Mireaux offers substantial evidence to the effect that the identification of Charles with his dynasty was a current concept as late as 1015. He avers further (although Menéndez-Pidal considers his reasoning oversubtle) that a line in the Old Norse parallel to the dream in laisse 186 of Digby-23 refers directly to the capture of Charles of Lorraine and therefore must have been included in a version of the *Chanson de Roland* which was circulating shortly after 991.[18] The line reads (Aebischer's translation): "Le roi Charlemagne est vaincu, et jamais par la suite il ne sera digne de porter la couronne en France."[19]

However, the primary historical evidence favoring the probability of a revision toward the end of the tenth century is the description in laisse 110 of the geographical extent of France over which the storm and eclipse portend the death of Roland. The France described here has been shown to fall within the confines of ancient Neustria, and conforms with the France of the end of the dynasty, with a capital at Laon, after Lorraine was attached to the Ottonian empire.[20] It is significant that laisse 110 is not only one of the focal narrative points of the 66 pattern, but, as will later be shown, occupies a dominant arithmetic position as well. It would be reasonable to suppose that the laisse was invented at the same time as the 66 pattern, for it is a laisse of transition which simply conveys the jongleur's comment and contributes nothing to the advancement of the narrative. As such it is of the type which serves for that kind of "stuffing" which is always needed to fill out or point up an arithmetic pattern.[21]

It is also to be noted that lines 1444-45 of this laisse seem to imply that the storm and earthquake presage the end of the world, which was generally expected to occur at the year 1000.

The inferences to be drawn from the foregoing discussion are as follows: Since, in using the number 11, which is dominant in the arithmetic pattern as a symbol for Roland's excessive fortitude, the poet indicates a desire to stress the *Démesure* motif above all others, and since the narrative points in the *Démesure* set stress Olivier's participation in the poem, it is highly probable that the revision in which the arithmetic pattern was incorporated was the same as that made to accommodate the inclusion of Olivier. It is reasoned further that, since laisse 110 attributed to the end of the Carolingian dynasty is a focal laisse in the pattern, and since the period of the end of the dynasty coincides with the period of the invention of Olivier, it is likely that the revision in which Olivier was introduced, that in which the arithmetic pattern was introduced and that made at the end of the dynasty, were one and the same revision.

Corollary to an assumption that the 66 pattern was invented at the same time that Olivier was created is the further assumption that this version of the Roland story was a written one, and that the revisionist of the end of the eleventh century who invented the 91 pattern when the Baligant story was added used the older written version as the basis for his new composition.[22] Otherwise, it would have to be presumed that the sequence of the laisses in which the 66 pattern has been retained, and which comprises over sixty percent of the total of the Oxford version, was preserved intact during almost a century of oral transmission.

It should not be cause for wonder that an early written version of an epic poem and its later revision manifest the stylistic traits of oral poetry which are so characteristic of the *Chanson de Roland,* for the oral versions were no doubt the only models

for nonhagiographic narrative which the poet had at his disposition. The studies of Milman Parry and Albert Lord on the
Homeric epic and the twentieth-century South Slavic epics, as
well as those of Jean Rychner on the French, have demonstrated
beyond question the function of formulaic expressions in oral
poetry.[23] Yet even in the *Vie de Saint Alexis*, whose written
origin has never been questioned, formulaic expressions similar
to those of the French epic, when counted by a seminar group
at the Ohio State University, were found to be equally as
numerous as they are in the *Roland*. In another instance, a
computer comparison of the formulaic expressions in the
anonymous twelfth-century *Siège de Barbaste* with those in the
thirteenth-century rhymed version by Adenet le Roi conducted
by Joseph Duggan showed, rather surprisingly, that while forty-
five percent of the lines of the oral work contained formulas, in
the late written revision, the count was only reduced to thirty
percent.[24]

Nor should the narrative inconsistencies of the Roland be
considered an indication that a revision was not written, for,
after all, every manuscript extant is in some measure a "written"
revision, and in every one inconsistencies abound. That they did
indeed originate in oral renditions is not questioned, but, probably from respect for time-honored passages, subsequent re-
arrangements seem to have tended to leave intact large blocks
of the narrative and to introduce a minimum of change to
accommodate new material. Thus it becomes increasingly evident that the oral style of the narrative genre, once crystalized,
continued to be imitated, both in writing and in oral renditions,
long after the functional purpose of the stylistic traits was viable.

It should be noted, however, that the postulation of a written
version need not preclude the possibility that numerous oral
renditions were also circulating, some stemming directly from
the written version, others perhaps reflecting versions antedating
the written form. Indeed, that marked diversion between manuscript *O* and all other manuscripts may well be accounted for
in just this way. Thus, while the Oxford manuscript would
manifest but two revisions, both written, one at the end of the

tenth century and the other at the end of the eleventh, other manuscripts, such as *n, V4, V7,* and so forth, would reflect the accretions and suppressions of an untold number of oral performances.

Charlemagne and the Twelve Peers

Since the 91 pattern necessitates the inclusion of Baligant matter, on the evidence of Henri Grégoire's identification of the events of the Baligant episode as a reflection of the expedition of 1085 against Alexius Commenius, this pattern could not have been invented earlier than that date.[25] The good correlation between the symbolic interpretation of the dominant numbers of the pattern and the characterization of Charles in the Baligant episode renders the probability high that the Baligant revisionist invented the 91 pattern.

In the set of points in the 66 pattern which develops Charlemagne's absence as a factor in the catastrophe, it is the fact of the king's absence and the prediction of his belated return which seem to be stressed. In this connection it is to be noted that the vengeance of which Turpin foretells in laisse 132 is not the conquest of the pagan king Baligant, but the chasing off of the remnants of Marsile's army: Turpin says quite simply, "If the king comes, he can avenge us; the Spaniards must not return from here happy" (lines 1744, 1745). Although in these particular laisses there would seem to be no very cogent evidence of intent to characterize Charles as the weak and aged king who would be identified with his waning dynasty, it must certainly be said that the sober and realistic acts of Charles in the 66 pattern are sharply in contrast with the flamboyant deeds of vengeance and conquest which constitute the dominant motif of the 91 pattern. In the latter version Charles has become the myth of Charlemagne, the Holy Roman Emperor and conqueror of the pagan, evoked from the distant past to inspire the Christian world in the great venture of the twelfth century, the crusade for the conquest of Jerusalem. The revision to accommodate the inclusion of the Baligant episode has, in the words of Menéndez-Pidal, transformed "la tragique épopée de Roland en un roman 'moralisateur,' au goût des esprits les plus candides, insatiable dans le châtiment du méchant et la plus haute exaltation du bon" (p. 126).

The association of Charles with the number thirteen, as the Christian leader of the twelve peers analogous with Christ and the twelve apostles, is, of course, essential to the metaphoric significance of the 91 pattern. However, whether this association was already established in the tradition, or whether it was the exclusive invention of the revisionist who conceived the pattern is not certain. It is true, of course, that the Old Norse version, in which the twelve peers are compared with the apostles, and the *Pèlerinage de Charlemagne*, where Charles, the leader of Christendom, is explicitly mentioned as the thirteenth, are both presumed to postdate Digby-23, and thus would be subject to the influence of the Oxford *Roland*. Nevertheless, it is to be born in mind that, in the Oxford text, there is no direct statement that Charles was the thirteenth and no overt attempt to compare the twelve peers with the apostles. So to assume that the complete allegory in the *Pèlerinage* and the analogy in the Old-Norse version stemmed directly from Digby-23 would necessitate the further assumption that there was widespread knowledge and understanding of the details and metaphoric significance of the 91 pattern. Such may have been the case, but the possibility should not be ruled out that specific mention of Charles as the thirteenth may have occurred in a prototype common to all three versions, most likely in the form of an oral rendition circulating toward the end of the eleventh century.

In so far as the conception of the peers as a body of twelve is concerned, the *Nota Emilianense*, written between 1065 and 1075, stands as evidence that this was not the invention of the Baligant revisionist. It is especially to be noted that the *Nota* evidences no intent to compare the group of peers with the twelve apostles, but specifically explains their number as deriving from the apportionment of their service to the king in correspondence with the twelve months of the year. Menéndez-

Pidal states that mention of such monthly service by a group of twelve is not found in any other French *chanson de geste* known, and expresses the opinion that it was also not the invention of a Spanish *juglar* (p. 397).[26]

Ménendez-Pidal discusses the possibilities of assigning a date to the conception of the heroes who died at Roncevaux as a body of twelve peers (pp. 285–86, 370–72). In the royal annals, those who were killed in the battle were simply called *palatini*, i.e., members of the royal household charged with various types of personal service to the king; no fixed number of them is specified. As examples of the posts which the *palatini*, also called the *fideles* or the *aulici*, customarily occupied are to be mentioned that of the *camerarius*, or master of the king's chamber and treasurer, the *senescalus* or maître d'hôtel (this was the function of Eggihardus, mentioned by Eginhard in the *Vita Karoli Magni*), the *comes stabuli* or chief of the cavalry, and the *comes palatii* or *coms palatinus*, who presided over the tribunal of the palace when the king was absent. The *palatini* in general sat at the palace tribunal in judicial cases reserved for the king.

In Carolingian times, the adjective *pars* (equal) denoted the great men of the realm, equal among themselves for their titles of nobility, but with no special assignment of service to the king. In the year 939, a group of nobles designated the *pares Francorum* revolted against Louis IV, d'Outremer, a historical incident which gave rise ultimately to the theme of *Renaut de Montauban*, in which twelve peers swear to kill Charlemagne.

Menéndez-Pidal remarks that, according to Emile Mireaux, the institution of the *pares curiae*—as a body of feudal vassals or peers, usually twelve in number, who assisted the suzerain in courts of justice—is attested as well-established in the north of France by the mid-eleventh century (p. 168n.). Menéndez-Pidal poses the question: Can one assign a date as remote as the end of the tenth century or the beginning of the eleventh to "la substitution, dans la *Chanson de Roland*, de ces pairs féodaux, chargés de fonctions judiciaires, aux palatins carolingiens?" He answers: "Nous ignorons complètement si cette modification a pu intervenir dans le poème a la même époque que la création du personnage d'Olivier, ou postérieurement."

The problem is, however, that nowhere in the Oxford *Roland* are the 12 peers mentioned in connection with any judicial function. The members of the various councils, both pagan and Christian, are mainly called *baruns* (lines 169, 180, 275, 536, 779, 877, etc.) or *humes* (lines 20, 79, 502, etc.) and more rarely *dux et cuntes* (line 14) or *jugeors* (line 3699). It is especially to be noted that, at the council in which Roland "judged" Ganelon as emissary to Marsile, when, in laisse 18, Olivier volunteers to take the place of Roland, Charles tells him to keep quiet declaring that neither Roland nor Olivier may go; then he adds: "*Par ceste barbe que veez blancheier,/Li duze per mar i serunt jugez!*" Thus Charlemagne seems to conceive *li duze per* as a body apart from the council. Furthermore, although some of the *duze per* are present at the council, not all members of the council are members of the group of twelve. Ganelon, for example, although a council member, considers himself distinct from the twelve when he says that, for what Roland has done to him, he will love neither him nor Olivier because he is Roland's friend and that he defies the 12 peers because they love Roland so much: "*Li duze per, por so qu'il l'aiment tante, / Desfi les ci, sire, vostre veiant*" (lines 325, 326). Thus the function of the 12 peers seems to be simply fighting, as good vassals and *franc chevalier*, and their designation *per* would seem to imply the sense of the *pares Francorum* of the early tenth century, i.e., the great nobles of the kingdom, equal in title and, in this case, loyal to the king, but not designated as a body for any particular service. Such would also be the sense of the term as it is used in line 285, where, with reference to Ganelon, it is said: "*Tant par fut bels tuit ses per l'en esguardent*," and in line 362, where Ganelon tells his retainers to greet in his name "*Pinabel, mun ami e mun per.*"

With respect to Mireaux's findings, then, it should be emphasized that the term *palatini* as employed in the royal annals with reference to those who died in the battle was hardly meant to connote anything more than "members of the king's household," without especial stress on their judicial function. Nor does there seem to be any reason to insist that the concept of the peers in the *Roland* as a body of twelve which performs no judicial function had to derive *from* the concept of the twelve judicial *pares curiae*. It would seem more to the point to inquire why the body of the *pares curiae* numbered twelve, and whether there is any connection between the choice of this number and the custom mentioned in the *Nota* which has to do with the apportionment of service to the king over twelve months of the year. That some such monthly service could just as well have been antecedent to the limitation of the judicial body to twelve is a possibility which need not be precluded by the rigid chronology of the historical evidence.

It is to be noted furthermore that mention of the 12 peers occurs with much higher frequency in the Roncevaux episode than it does in the Baligant part of the story, and is, in fact, so inextricably interwoven in the fabric of the earlier version that it is hard to imagine that the Baligant revisionist would have set it in, for, as will later be shown, he was not prone to make extensive changes in the actual text of the material he had inherited. Thus, in the absence of conclusive evidence to the contrary, it can be assumed that the concept of the peers as a body of 12 was either the invention of the Olivier revisionist or already present in the material which he revised. The inference would then be that the Baligant revisionist, having inherited the concept of the twelve from his predecessor, chose the number thirteen as the arithmetic symbol for Charlemagne, but could very well have been influenced in his choice by an interpretation current in the *Roland* tradition toward the end of the eleventh century which associated the group of twelve and Charles as the thirteenth with Christ and the twelve apostles.

1. Ramón Menéndez-Pidal (*La Chanson de Roland et la tradition épique des Francs,* pp. 16, 122, 228) cites Albert Pauphilet, "Sur la *Chanson de Roland,*" *Romania* 59 (1933): 183–96.

2. "Etudes d'anthroponymie ancienne française," *PMLA* 58 (1943): 589–

93. Cf. Ernst Robert Curtius (*European Literature and the Latin Middle Ages*, pp. 167–82 and 536–37), who discusses the antecedents of the topos in classical antiquity and the Latin Middle Ages.

3. Rita Lejeune, "La naissance du couple littéraire 'Roland et Olivier,'" in *Mélanges Henri Grégoire*, II, of the *Annuaire de l'Institut de Philologie et d'Histoire Orientales et Slaves* 10 (1950): 372–401. Madame Lejeune's findings have been checked by Paul Aebischer, "Les trois mentions plus anciennes du couple 'Roland et Olivier,'" *Revue belge de philologie et d'histoire* 30 (1952): 657–75. Menéndez-Pidal gives a bibliography and a critical evaluation of the numerous studies treating the invention of the character Olivier and the anthroponymic attestions (pp. 336–65).

4. "Contributi alla storia dell'epopea e del romanzo medievale; L'onomastica italiana e l'epopea carolingia," *Romania* 18 (1889) : 9.

5. Menéndez-Pidal summarizes the general reaction to Spitzer's proposal (pp. 349, 350). Notable among the neo-traditionalists who are in agreement is Jules Horrent, *La Chanson de Roland dans les littératures française et espagnole au moyen âge*, pp. 292–97, et passim. Menéndez-Pidal (p. 350) cites, as an acceptable resolution of the individualist and neo-traditionalist views, the opinion of Maurice Delbouille (*Sur la genèse de la Chanson de Roland*, pp. 162–63), who avers that only a fine poem in the vernacular, conceived by a cleric in conformity with the old scholarly topos, *sapientia et fortitudo,* could achieve the renown revealed by the onomastic vogue, and that this success entrained not only baptisms with the names Roland-Olivier, but also the fictional tombs at Blaye, false relics, local legends, apocryphal documents of authorization, and finally, at the beginning of the twelfth century, the "œuvre maîtresse" of Turoldus.

6. Paul Aebischer, *Rolandiana et Oliveriana: Recueil d'études sur les chansons de geste*. This collection reproduces a series of Aebischer's articles published during the period from 1949 to 1967. Of especial interest to the current study is the article on pp. 141–73, "Trois personnages en quête d'auteurs: Roland, Olivier, Aude. Contribution à la génétique de la *Chanson de Roland*," which first appeared in *Festschrift Walter Baetke*, ed. Kurt Rudolph, Rolf Heller, and Ernest Walter (Weimar, 1966).

7. See the discussion of Menéndez-Pidal, (p. 356), and of Aebischer (*Rolandiana et Oliveriana*, p. 156), of the signatures to a document in the *Cartulaire de Saint-Victor de Marseille* discovered by Madame Lejeune, "La naissance," p. 377.

8. *Girart de Vienne Chanson de Geste.*

9. Aebischer (*Rolandiana et Oliveriana*, p. 158) cites the edition of C. R. Unger, *Karlamagnus saga ok kappa hans* (Christiania, 1860), and states that the material treating the matter of *Girard de Vienne* is to be found in chapters 34, 35, and 38–42 of the first branch of this text. Cf. René Louis, *Girart, comte de Vienne dans les chansons de geste,* (Paris, 1947). In regard

to the ascription of the *Karlamagnus saga* to the fourteenth century, Aebischer (*Rolandiana et Oliveriana*, p. 274), cites Unger, p. xxvii, and also the *Katalog over den arnamagnoeanske Handskriftsamling* (Copenhaven, 1888) 1:148, 149.

10. Aebischer, *Rolandiana et Oliveriana*, p. 159.

11. See note 9 above.

12. Aebischer, *Rolandiana et Oliveriana*, pp. 158, 159.

13. See note 30 of chapter 2 above.

14. Jean Frappier, *Les chansons de geste du cycle de Guillaume d'Orange*, 1:63.

15. Hippolyte Delehaye, *Les passions des martyrs et les genres littéraires*, pp. 236–315.

16. Curtius discusses the problem of *fortitudo* in connection with the rise of the crusading spirit in the eleventh and twelfth centuries (pp. 536, 537).

17. Menéndez-Pidal: "Tout au contraire, la Muse tragique de l'épopée, étrangère à cette inspiration religieuse et savante, a de tout temps compris que le héros n'est précisément un héros que pour n'être ni parfait, ni sage, ni modéré" (p. 340).

18. Emile Mireaux, *La Chanson de Roland et l'histoire de France*, pp. 130, 133, 134.

19. Paul Aebischer, *Rolandiana borealia*, p. 228.

20. Cf. Ferdinand Lot, "Etudes sur les légendes épiques françaises," *Romania* 54 (1928): 374–76; Robert Fawtier, *La Chanson de Roland*, pp. 192–98, 211; and the summary by Menéndez-Pidal (pp. 335, 336), of the address of René Louis before the First International Congress of the *Société Roncesvals* at Poitier in 1959.

21. See note 25 of chapter 2, above.

22. Cf. the opinion of Delbouille, note 5, above.

23. Cf. Jean Rychner, *La Chanson de geste*; Milman Parry, *Les formules et la métrique d'Homère*; and Albert B. Lord, *The Singer of Tales*.

24. Cf. Joseph C. Duggan, "Formulaic Language in the Old-French Epic Poems *Le Siège de Barbastre and Beuvon de Conmarchis*" (Ph.D. diss., The Ohio State University, 1964).

25. See note 6 of chapter 2, above.

26. One might inquire whether the twelve captains appointed by David to serve one month each might not have suggested this concept. See I Chronicles 24:25.

The Inventors at Work

Chapter Four

The Roncevaux and the Baligant Material

FIGURE 12 ILLUSTRATES the manner in which the two arithmetic patterns manifested in Digby-23 were combined and shows how, on the pattern treating the Roncevaux material down to the point of Roland's death, there was superimposed the 91 pattern embracing the whole of the Oxford version with the Baligant episode included. The reworking needed to accommodate the Baligant material may be compared with the remodeling of a house when a new wing is added. Thus, in the general reconstruction of the facade, the major corridor between the old building and the new—that band in brackets of 91 laisses between the final destruction of the rearguard and the vengeance of Charles—was used as the basis of the new structural unit to replace the 66 bracket. The pattern of the new unit, carried out in imitation of the old, was then fitted, with more success than might be expected, over major points of jointure still retained in the original structure.

It will be recalled that, in the 66 pattern, the set of brackets treating the Absence of Charles at laisse 66 and Turpin's prediction of his return for vengeance and burial at 132 does not continue to the third narrative point, which would occur at laisse 198. The obvious reason for this defect is that, at a point before laisse 198, the continuity of the laisses treating the concluding events of the Roncevaux story was disrupted when they were interspersed among those of the new Baligant material.

For the moment it will be assumed that, if all mention of the battle with Baligant and the taking of Zaragoza are deleted from the Oxford version, what remains will be "Roncevaux material"

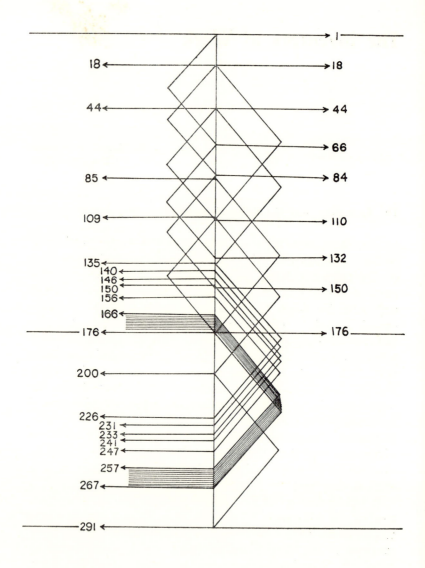

Fig. 12. The 66 and 91 patterns.

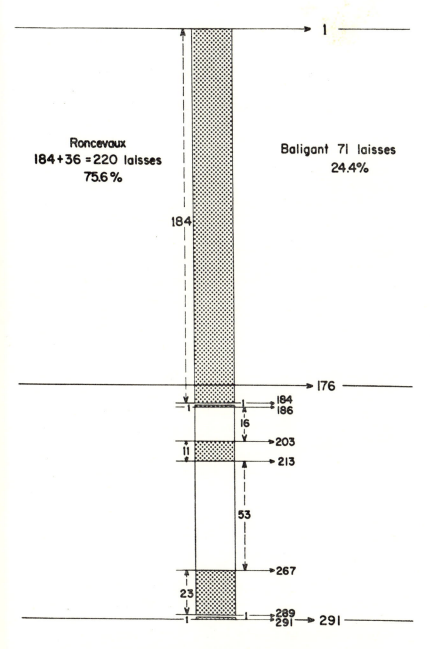

Fig. 13. Distribution of Roncevaux and Baligant material.

shown in figure 13 in hatched blocks.[1] Thus, the Roncevaux story is seen to continue without interruption down through laisse 184, the last of a group of three parallel laisses where the French rest for the night after having dispersed the army of Marsile. Charles, his heart heavy with grief for the loss of Roland, finally falls into a sleep tormented by two prophetic dreams, which God sends to him by the angel Gabriel. The first, in laisse 185, seems to be a prognostication of Charlemagne's coming battle with Baligant, and as such, will be classified for the moment as Baligant matter. The second dream, in laisse 186, foretells the trial of Ganelon, which appertains to the Roncevaux story. In laisse 187, the scene switches sharply to Marsile, as he nurses his wound in Zaragoza, and Baligant is mentioned for the first time in laisse 188. From here through laisse 202, the narrative treats the preparations of the Saracens for battle with Charles. In laisse 203, the thread of the narrative breaks again, and the scene shifts back to Charlemagne as he awakens on the morning after his dreams. The emperor and the French mount and return to Roncevaux, and from this point through laisse 213, Charles laments the death of Roland, has the French soldiers buried on the field of battle, and has the bodies of Roland, Olivier, and Turpin prepared for burial. In the section between 214 and 266 are related the events of the battle with Baligant and the taking of Zaragoza, and, in the long laisse 267, Charles establishes a garrison at Zaragoza, leaves the city taking along the captive queen Bramimonde, takes Narbonne, and passes on to Bordeaux, where he deposits the horn on the altar of Saint Seurin. Then, crossing the Gironde, he lays to rest the bodies of Roland, Olivier, and Turpin in sarcophagi in Saint Romain, and thence goes on to Aix, where he calls his judges to begin the trial of Ganelon. In laisses 268 and 269, Aude is told of the death of Roland and dies on the spot, and the section from laisse 270 through 289 treats the trial and execution of Ganelon and his relatives. In laisse 290, Bramimonde is baptized and takes a Christian name, and in the final laisse 291, the emperor is called by Gabriel to help King Vivien in the city of

Imphe, which is besieged by pagans. Charles does not wish to go; his life is full of trials. His eyes fill with tears, and he pulls his white beard. And thus ends the epic which Turoldus recounts.

By this distribution, of the total of 291 laisses, 71 treat exclusively Baligant matter, leaving 220 for the material dealing with the Roncevaux story. Of the latter, two laisses treat both Baligant and Roncevaux matter: laisse 267, of which seven lines (3676–82) tell of the garrisoning of Zaragoza and Charlemagne's departure from the city with Bramimonde, and laisse 291, where one line (3990) refers to Bramimonde. If all of the Baligant matter is extracted, and the remaining laisses are left exactly in the sequence in which they occur in Digby-23, the Roncevaux narrative will progress in logical order.

Thus, the French rest after chasing off the remnants of Marsile's army and Charles dreams of the trial of Ganelon (186). At dawn, Charles and the French return to Roncevaux where Charles laments Roland, buries the French soldiers, and prepares the heroes for burial (203–13). Night passes and the day dawns clear (line 3675 of laisse 267), the French force their way through Narbonne (line 3683 of laisse 267) and proceed to Bordeaux, Blaye, and thence to Aix. From this point, the story of Aude's death and the trial continues as in Digby-23, with the exception of the reference to Bramimonde in laisse 290 and line 3990 of laisse 291.

When the matter pertaining to the battle with Baligant is simply deleted from Digby-23, a fairly acceptable version of the aftermath of the Roncevaux disaster remains. There is reasonable ground for assuming, however, that such a version does not represent the exact form of the original version of the 66 pattern and that the Baligant revisionist changed, in a few minor areas, the text of the Olivier revisionist, which he was using as the basis of his new composition.

It is the view of Menéndez-Pidal that the recital in laisse 185 of the dream which seems to predict the battle with Baligant has been revised from an older version dating from a time when the Baligant material had not been invented (p. 334).[2] He maintains that the original version would have referred to the rebellion of the Saxons, which was very probably the historical reason for Charlemagne's hasty departure from Spain without taking the city of Zaragoza, and he points out that direct reference is made to this revolt in the lament of laisse 209, where Charles asks who will lead his army against such a power, now that Roland is dead (pp. 199–202).[3]

It is worthy of note, furthermore, that the Old Norse version of laisses 185 and 186 refers to the dream of 186 as the "third" dream, thus implying that the matter of laisse 186 treats two dreams. Aebischer marks the division at the point comparable to the end of line 2541 of laisse 185 in the Oxford version.[4] The older form may thus have been that part between lines 2525 and 2541, and the remainder, including reference to Charlemagne's struggle with the lion, which seem to portend his individual battle with Baligant, would comprise the addition of the Baligant revisionist.[5] For this reason, it is assumed here that laisse 185 with lines 2542–54 deleted was included in the text of the 66 pattern.

Menéndez-Pidal maintains that Aude was created by the revisionist who invented Olivier, because the poet wished to soften the warlike atmosphere of the story with accents of delicate sensibility and human pathos (pp. 366, 367). That the creator of Olivier manifests delicate sensibilities in matters of *compagnonnage* there is no question. However, so far as the episode of Aude's death is concerned, with all due respect to the profound perspicacity of Professor Menéndez-Pidal, it could just as well be argued here that the particularly romantic quality of her story is more in keeping with that taste of the cultural ambience of which Bramimonde was a product, and which was soon to produce the twelfth-century romance, than with the serious and heroic tone of the *sapientia-fortitudo* conflict.

Reason on a more functional level for doubting the existence of the Aude episode prior to the Baligant revision is the fact that the two laisses in which her death is related are introduced into the version of Digby-23 without transition and as an abrupt interruption of another narrative in a manner which is consistently characteristic of the Baligant revisionist. At the end of laisse 267, after the burial of the heroes, it is stated that, when Charles arrives at Aix, he sends messengers to assemble his council of *jugeors*, and the last line of laisse 267 then states: "Now begins the trial of Ganelon."[6]

Laisse 268 begins with a typical reprise: Charles has returned from Spain to Aix; he goes up in his palace to his hall and has Aude brought to him.[7] From this point, the remainder of laisse 268 and all of 269 are devoted exclusively to Aude and nowhere mention Ganelon's trial. It is not until laisse 270 that the thread of the trial story is taken up again: "Charles has returned to Aix. Ganelon, the felon, is in chains in the fortress in front of the palace," and so forth.[8] Thus it can be seen that the flow of the old narrative has been cut to insert new material in exactly the same manner as that which has so often been observed between laisses 187 and 188, which leaves Charles dreaming and sleeping to switch to Marsile seeking the aid of Baligant, and between 202 and 203, which leaves Baligant calling up the pagans to return to Charles awakening the morning after his dreams. The trait is perhaps most flagrantly evident in the long interruption after laisse 213, where the heroes are prepared for a burial which will not take place until laisse 267, after the battle with Baligant. Thus it would seem that, on the grounds of stylistic traits, it can well be concluded that the two laisses which recount the death of Aude were inserted by the Baligant revisionist.[9] Whether or not he also inserted the three lines (1719–21) of laisse 130, where Olivier mentions her in the horn dispute (the only other mention of Aude in the whole text), is a matter in which stylistic analysis offers no aid, and judgement of this question is held in abeyance.

Finally, Menéndez-Pidal expresses the opinion that the conclusion of the version of the Roland story prior to the Baligant revision can be reconstructed from the versions of other extant manuscripts and should be substituted for the last two laisses of Digby-23, which occur only in the Oxford version (pp. 126–29). Laisse 290 tells of the baptism of Bramimonde, hitherto

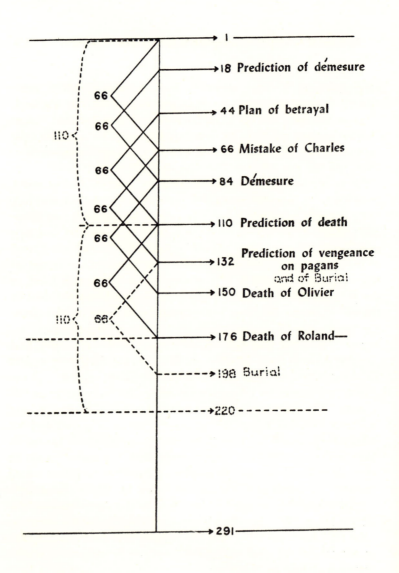

Fig. 14. The original 66 pattern.

classified as Baligant material, and laisse 291, after further
mention of Bramimonde, tells of the angel's appeal to Charles
to assist King Vivien in his defense of Imphe in the land of Bire.
Although Menéndez-Pidal does not give his views in the matter,
conceivably, the reconstructed version which he proposes would
also occupy two laisses. The first, from manuscripts *V4, C, V7,*
and *P,* would comprise an address by Charles to his barons
immediately after the execution of Ganelon to the effect that he
is now satisfied, thanks to the death of the one who caused him
the loss of Roland and the twelve peers, and that he will never
again see nephew (*V4*) or the twelve peers (*C, V7, P*). In the
final laisse, Charles would mount to his hall and call his barons
(*C, V7*), take leave of them and offer them presents (*T, L*),
and embrace them tenderly and sigh at the memory of Roland.
The barons would return home and Charles would remain alone,
sad and dejected.

In table 2 of the appendix is shown the manner in which the
laisses which are proposed for the termination of the original
story of the 66 pattern compare with those of Digby-23. In
figure 14 it can be seen that the total story of the 66 pattern
comprised 220 laisses, and it will be noted that the burial of
Roland and the heroes now occurs in laisse 198 (Oxford version
267), the missing point in the set of brackets marking the
participation of Charlemagne. Thus the king's theme is completed with the absence of Charles at laisse 66, Turpin's prediction of his return to avenge and bury at laisse 132, and the
burial at laisse 198. It is to be noted further that the final point
of this set of brackets falls on a number which, like the other two,
is divisible by both 6 and 11; that, with the inclusion of laisse
198, the 66 pattern comprises nine narrative points, which,
together with the beginning and the end, give a total of eleven
points in all; and that the total of 220 laisses is also divisible by
11. The intervals between the points now fall into the pattern
44:22; 44:22; 44:22, plus a coda of 22 which exactly accommo-
dates the trial of Ganelon and the two reconstructed laisses of
the conclusion. When the intervals of 44:22 are combined, the

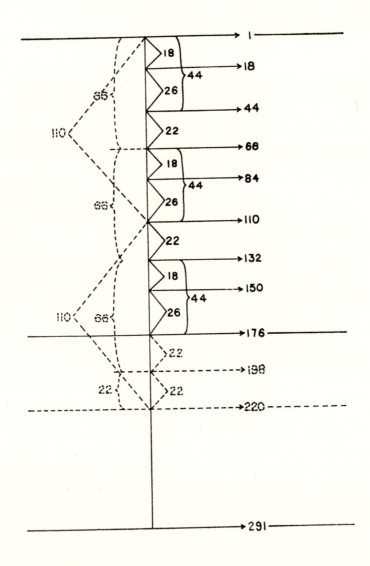

Fig. 15. The original 66 pattern (reverse).

overall pattern of the poem becomes 66:66:66:22. (See figure 15.)

The Original 66 Pattern

If the series $66+66+66+22=220$ is divided through by its smallest unit, 22, the result will be $3+3+3+1=10$. It will be recalled that, in medieval reasoning, the numbers 10, 100, 1000, and so forth, were mystically the equivalent of unity, probably because, in the decimal system of counting, the next highest numeral above nine represented a return to unity, or a new beginning, with the number one now in the next decimal column to the left. From the evidence offered by the *Alexis* and the *Divine Comedy*, it would seem that it was a custom with poets who used structural arithmetic metaphor to base their patterns on some formula for a tripartite division of unity which would, in their view, express arithmetically the paradox of the unity of the three in one of the Christian Trinity. This paradox must indeed have posed a problem, for, since medieval arithmetic preferred to deal with integers, there was simply no way to make an even three-way division of ten or any of its powers.

The poet of the *Alexis* accomplished the feat rather well by including a count of syllables in his pattern and thereby reducing the fractional difference to a negligible minimum. Thus he divided the one hundred stanzas which related the events of the saint's life on earth into three parts, each comprising $33\frac{1}{3}$ 5-line stanzas, a formula for unity which in algebraic terms would be $3(33A+\frac{A}{3})=100$, when $A=1$. Then, by using a ten-syllable line with caesura after the fourth, he contrived to have the soul of Alexis reach his heavenly Lord at the two-thirds point at *syllable* 34 of stanza 67 (that is, at syllable 3334 of a total of 5,000), which was as nearly as he could come to expressing the concept "two-thirds" in a decimal pattern with the integers at his disposal.[10]

The formula which Dante used for the *Divine Comedy* was slightly different: From the total of one hundred cantos, he simply isolated one canto for his introduction and divided the remaining 99 into three equal parts, thus creating a structure $1+33+33+33=100$, which would be stated algebraically $A+3(33A)=100$, when $A=1$.

The arithmetic reasoning of the poet of the 66 pattern in the *Roland* was probably as follows: He wished to employ the number 11 to symbolize the concept "excess," and he wished also to base his composition on some arithmetic expression of the tripartite unity of the Christian Trinity. For this he chose the structure $3+3+3+1=10$, which can be stated algebraically $3(3A)+A=10$, when $A=1$. The story he wanted to tell would require some two hundred laisses, more or less. If he multiplied his base formula through by 11, the result would be a structure in the form $33+33+33+11=110$, but this would only provide about half of the units he needed. Therefore, he multiplied through again by 2, and so obtained the structure $66+66+66+22=220$, which would accommodate the material very nicely and allow leeway for jongleurs' comments and repetitions at important points. He was doubtlessly very much pleased with the results he had obtained so far, for he now had a form which would express symbolically both unity and excess: unity in the base formula and excess in abundance through multiplication by the double of 11. Furthermore, in the sections of 66 units, he had not only a multiple of 11, but also its aggregate. Finally, the traditional implications of evil in the number 66, which now turned out to be the aggregate of the number of excess, must indeed have confirmed his belief in the symbolic meaning of numbers.

The poet then decided to use the section $66+66+66=198$ for the events of the hero's tragedy through to the moment of burial, and to reserve the unit 22 for a coda in which justice would be accomplished. It is to be noted here that the structure which the poet of the *Roland* chose for the story of his hero parallels very closely that which the poet of the *Alexis* chose for that of the saint, where, of the divisions $33\frac{1}{3}+33\frac{1}{3}+33\frac{1}{3}+25=125$, the part $33\frac{1}{3}+33\frac{1}{3}+33\frac{1}{3}=100$ was reserved for the events of the life of the saint up through preparation for burial, and the coda of twenty-five stanzas was devoted to the apotheosis.

Having now obtained three major divisions of 66 laisses for Roland's deeds, death, and burial, the poet then placed at nine points within his composition three thematic sets, comprising three laisses each, spaced at intervals of 66 laisses, which would stress the three major factors of the hero's tragedy: *Démesure,* Betrayal, and the King's Absence. The points of one set were already determined by the major divisions, and, since the burial would have to occur at laisse 198, and would also have to be performed by the king, this set was assigned to the king's participation: Absence at 66, Prediction of Return for Burial at 132, and Burial at 198. Then, since laisse 110 was both mystically the equivalent of eleven and the halfway point of the total composition as well, it would be appropriate for a set of brackets to fit into this point. However, while the end points of such a set could be made to fall on the Betrayal and the Death of Roland, at laisses 44 and 176, there was, in the area of laisse 110, no outstanding event which would be suitable for the theme. In this place he would have to insert a jongleur's comment, with some portentous prediction, and so he created laisse 110, where the death of Roland was foretold by a storm and eclipse over the whole of that France which the poet knew—France at the end of the Carolingian dynasty. It is to be noted that, within the total of 220 laisses, the Betrayal set, which is the basic set of the poem and the essence of Roland's story, is absolutely symmetrical having its midpoint at the half with an equal distribution of sections of 66 and 44 on either side forming the pattern $44 + 66 + 66 + 44 = 220$.

The poet now had one set of brackets which fell on points divisible by six and eleven, and another set on points divisible by eleven. It would be suitable to make the third set fit into points divisible by six. Since many such points were available, the poet's decision to start the set with laisse 18 was probably determined simply by the order of the narrative. In this manner the *Démesure* set was created, with Olivier's Prediction of *Démesure* at 18, the horn dispute at 84, and Olivier's death at 150.

The task which remained was simply one of telling the story

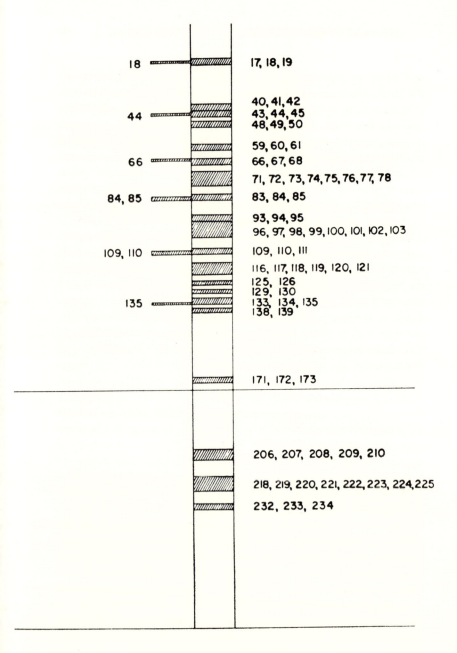

Fig. 16. Parallel laisses.

and filling out the material so that the narrative would fit properly on the brackets. Filling was no problem, for it could always be done by using parallel or similar laisses with different assonance, as the jongleurs were accustomed to do, both as a means of being sure that the wandering attention of their audience would not miss an important point in the story, and also simply as a demonstration of their rhyming dexterity and ability to make variations on a theme.[11] The inventor of the 66 pattern, who doubtlessly could recite on demand many versions of the story he wished to revise, would, when he started his composition, have had at his disposal a number of such laisses inherited from his predecessors; and, since he was himself an excellent poet, he could easily create more. By their judicious placement, like building blocks around the armature of his arithmetic structure, he could achieve a variety of artistic effects and accomplish many poetic ends, such as smoothing transitions, heightening the high points of the action, slowing the narrative, and adding lyric tone to the pathetic passages. Indeed, it is primarily the arrangement of the parallel laisses which accounts for the effect of patterned texture so often remarked in the Oxford *Roland*. In figure 16, showing their distribution in the text, especially to be noted is the high incidence of their occurrence in the Roncevaux story as compared with that in the Baligant addition.

The 91 Pattern

When the mathematical structure of the 91 pattern is compared with that of the 66 pattern, which served as its model, it becomes evident that the pattern employed to reconstruct the older edifice manifests none of the arithmetic elegance of the original. The revisionist who added the Baligant episode and invented the 91 pattern obviously chose the number 13 for its capacity to signify Charlemagne in his mythical conception; but, as it will be recalled, the primary symbolic meaning of the number was inspired by the analogy of Charles and the twelve peers with Christ and the twelve apostles. This analogy, which must have been current at the end of the eleventh century and which probably stems from an oral version of the chanson, seems to have originated in popular superstition, since there is no indication that it could have been fostered in ecclesiastical tradition. The unit 91 was probably selected, in imitation of the 66 pattern, because it was the aggregate of 13 and the product of 13 times 7, but in many respects it was an unfortunate choice.

The overall structure of the pattern works out to $18+91+91+91=291$, a series which cannot be reduced to any underlying base structure such as that symbolizing the unity of Christian Trinity, since neither the number 91 nor its factors bears any arithmetic relation to the total of 291 laisses or the group of 18 laisses by which the three groups of 91 laisses are preceded. In addition, none of the points on which the brackets fall are divisible by the factors.

Perhaps the greatest defect of the 91 pattern, however, lies in the fact that 291 laisses are simply not sufficient for the requirements of the narrative. As can be seen from the abrupt manner with which the revisionist inserts his new material, there is no room for the necessary transitional laisses, and, furthermore, the framework is too limited to permit the inclusion of parallel or similar laisses with which the poet could have accented his story had he had the talent or inclination to do so. Finally, the exigencies of the pattern seem to have forced the poet to crowd too much narrative material into the individual laisses. This trait becomes increasingly noticeable toward the end of the poem, particularly in the important laisse 267 telling of the burial of the heroes, which as laisse 198 of the 66 pattern, had occupied a dominant position at the terminal point before the coda. In his effort to preserve this laisse as a narrative point in the new pattern, so that it made the set *Démesure* (85), Death of Roland (176), and Burial (267), the poet was constrained to include in it the quite unrelated material treating the garrison of Zaragoza and Charlemagne's departure with Bramimonde, but apparently found no room to explain what was done with the bodies of the three heroes while Charles was fighting the battle with Baligant. The general effect is similar to that of the motto THINK lettered by a sign painter who forgot to leave room for the *K*, and the audience is left with the unpleasant feeling that the author had to bring the story to a hasty conclusion because he had neither the time nor the space to do it justice. In summary, then, it must be said that the 91 pattern of the Baligant revision is, from a mathematical point of view, simply not interesting, and, from a poetic point of view, inadequate for the material.

The Genius of Digby-23

It thus becomes apparent that the architectonic form for which the Oxford *Roland* is famous owes its effect almost exclusively to what remains of the 66 pattern. The real "genius" of Digby-23 was not Turoldus—if Turoldus it was who invented Baligant —but the poet or poets, who, a century earlier, had invented Olivier and placed the story in the frame of a unity symbolizing the Christian Trinity, which, when raised by the number of Roland's excessive fortitude, resounded in the *tinnuli rhythmi* of a *Cantilena Rollandi*. The poet who created the 66 pattern was, as were the poet of the *Alexis* and Dante after him, a master of the *ars poetica* of structural arithmetic metaphor. If the "ringing rhythms" of his masterpiece are still heard today, it is because, in conferring numbered form on the microcosm which was his poem, he wished to imitate God's ordering of the great macrocosm, secure in the belief that the antiphonal vibrations of the numbers he chose would find accord with the numbers of that great silent harmony of time, motion, heavens, the stars, and all sorts of revolutions preexistent in the mind of the world-creating God.

---

1. Jules Horrent (*La Chanson de Roland dans la littérature française et espagnole au moyen âge*, pp. 105 ff. and 157 ff.) maintains that all Roland matter in Digby-23 not appertaining exclusively to the battle with Baligant and the taking of Zaragoza formed a part of the "original" *Chanson de Roland* of the early eleventh century. He classifies the Aude episode as a part of the earlier version (pp. 134–38).

2. For convenience of reference, laisse 185 is given here in full:

2525—Karles se dort cum hume traveillet.
 Seint Gabriel li ad Deus enveiet:
 L'empereür li cumandet a guarder.
 Li angles est tute noit a sun chef.
 Par avisium li ad anunciet
2530—D'une bataille ki encuntre lui ert:
 Senefiance l'en demustrat mult gref.
 Carles guardat amunt envers le ciel,
 Veit les tuneires e les venz e les giels
 E les orez, les merveillus tempez.
2535—E fous e flambes i est apareillez:
 Isnelement sur tute sa gent chet.
 Ardent cez hanstes de fraisne e de pumer
 E cez escuz jesqu'as bucles d'or mier,
 Fruissent cez hanstes de cez trenchanz espiez,
2540—Cruissent osbercs e cez helmes d'acer;
 En grant dulor i veit ses chevalers.
 Urs e leuparz les voelent puis manger,
 Serpenz e guivres, dragun e averser;
 Grifuns i ad, plus de trente millers:
2545—N'en i ad cel a Franceis ne s'agiet.
 E Franceis crient: "Carlemagne, aidez!"
 Le reis en ad e dulur e pitet;
 Aler i volt, mais il ad desturber:
 Devers un gualt uns granz leons li vient,
2550—Mult par ert pesmes e orguillus e fiers,
 Sun cors meïmes i asalt e requert
 E prenent sei a braz ambesdous por loiter;
 Mais ço ne set liquels abat ne quels chiet.
 Li empercre n'est mie esveillet.

3. Lines 2921–27:

 Encuntre mei revelerunt li Seisne
 E Hungre e Bugre e tante gent averse,
 Romain, Puillain e tuit icil de Palerne
 E cil d'Affrike e cil de Califerne,
 Puis entrerunt mes peines e mes suffraites.
 Ki guierat mes oz a tel poeste,
 Quant cil est morz ki tuz jurz nos cadelet?

4. Paul Aebischer, *Rolandiana borealia*; pp. 226–28, 282.

5. The Old Norse poet must have known two versions, the earlier, and the one with the Baligant addition, and was thus led to conclude that the addition was a second dream.

6. Lines 3698–704:

> Cume il est en sun paleis halçur,
> Par ses messages mandet ses jugeors,
> Baivers e Saisnes, Loherencs e Frisuns;
> Alemans mandet, si mandet Borguignuns
> E Peitevins e Normans e Bretuns,
> De cels de France des plus saives qui sunt.
> Dès ore cumencet le plait de Guenelun.

7. Lines 3705–8:

> Li empereres est repairet d'Espaigne
> E vient a Ais, al meillor sied de France;
> Muntet el palais, est venut en la sale.
> As li Alde venue, une bele damisele.

8. Lines 3734–36:

> Li emperere est repairet ad Ais.
> Guenes li fels, en caeines de fer,
> En la citet est devant le paleis.

9. It has been suggested in chapter 3, that the character Aude was developed in the "enfance" material of a primitive version of the *Girard de Vienne* epic. The Baligant revisionist would thus have borrowed her from the stories of the youth of Olivier and Roland which would have been circulating by the end of the eleventh century.

10. Cf. Eleanor Webster Bulatkin, "The Arithmetic Structure of the Old-French *Vie de Saint Alexis*," *PMLA* 74 (1959) : 499.

11. See note 25 of chapter 2, above.

The Provenience
of the Oxford "Roland"

IT IS FITTING TO ATTEMPT A SUMMATION of the ways in which this study purports to enlighten the provenience of the Oxford *Roland*, bearing in mind, of course, that in the present state of our knowledge assertions regarding the condition of the poem before Digby-23 cannot be definitive, for there are no earlier texts of a poem *qua* poem and external evidence is limited. Thus hypotheses can only be based on internal analyses and necessarily speculative reconstructions of poetic events now lost in time. In this respect, the arithmetic metaphor which has been proposed is no exception.

Essentially, it has been said that there are discernible in the Oxford version two arithmetic structures, an earlier one which was probably invented toward the beginning of the eleventh century and a later revision which was devised for the Oxford version of the beginning of the twelfth century. It is also posited that the numbers used in the structure were selected for their metaphoric significance, with the result that the pattern of the earlier version emphasized the excessive valor of Roland; that of the later, the vengeance of Charlemagne.

The evolution of the Roland matter is envisioned somewhat as follows: Between the early ninth century and about the beginning of the eleventh, jongleuresque poems were circulating which told of Roland's stand at Roncevaux. About the year 1000, a jongleur under clerical influence reviewed the material then in existence and constructed a new version incorporating the new character Olivier and embedding in the poem a numerical structure which reiterated in arithmetic metaphor the conflict between *sapientia* and *fortitudo*, which the clergy, in its desire to constrain the excessive warfare within the Christian community, wished emphasized. This version was thus sanctioned by the clergy and must have been written down at the time of composition and so preserved that it was available to the Oxford revisionist a century later.

Then at the beginning of the twelfth century, and again with the collaboration of the clergy, the old written version was reworked to express the changed attitude of the clergy toward militancy, an attitude inspired by the inception of the crusades. At this time the Baligant episode was added to permit a characterization of Charlemagne as the avenger of Christendom. The poet broke up the old number structure and superimposed a new one, and, as has been shown in chapter 4, he was not as accomplished in the art as was the poet of the original structure. This version is preserved in the Oxford manuscript.

In the meantime, throughout the eleventh century and later, other versions of the Roland story were circulating. These versions derived in part from the pre-Olivier story but at the same time borrowed freely from the written versions, which were perhaps being recited by a special line of jongleurs. It is possible that the other versions were transmitted orally until they came to be recorded in all of the manuscripts other than *O*. The present work treats only the line of provenience of the Oxford version. Other versions of the *Roland* corpus have not been examined for the presence of number structure; and, with the possible exception of the Latin *Pseudo-Turpin* or the *Carmen de prodicione Guenonis*, it is improbable that such a study would be fruitful.

Credence is lent to the proposal of this study by the fact that, at least during the period from the creation of the *Alexis* to the composition of the *Commedia Divina*, there was viable an aesthetic practice which sought to compose a poem so as to conceal within it an arithmetic structure with metaphoric intent. Since the postulated revisions of the *Chanson de Roland* fall roughly within this period of viability, the incorporation of such structures in the poem would reflect contemporaneous aesthetic tradition. It has also been demonstrated that the conception of arithmetic structuring and the metaphoric significance of the numbers employed are consonant with the number philosophy of the Middle Ages, itself the product of a tradition of great antiquity. Finally, the coherence of the constructs and their congruence with the obvious intent of the poem as well as with the evolving historic, aesthetic, and philosophic ambience, indicate a probability in favor of the postulation which is well beyond chance.

Of necessity the postulation of two levels of number structure in the Roland epic implies that there was clerical participation in its composition and dissemination and that the version of the year 1000 was written. Both implications are in conflict with the tendency of current neo-traditionalism to view medieval epic poetry as exclusively the product of an oral jongleuresque tradition which was entirely free of learned influence. However, it is exactly the weakness of the neo-traditionalist position that so large a portion of the argument, pro and con, uses as a point of departure the Oxford version of the *Chanson de Roland*. This text has obviously received so much attention because of its beauty and its renown, but ironically, by reason of its very excellence, it is a defective example of the kind of transmission which the neo-traditionalists justifiably posit as the rule for the general corpus of Old French epic material. Let it be said that the battle for the cause of the oral transmission of Old French epic poetry has been won; few scholars today would question the magnitude of the accomplishment. Let us now concede that, in the absence of evidence to the contrary, it is as arbitrary to insist that there was no written or clerical influence prior to the texts which happen to have survived as it is to argue that there was no such thing as oral transmission during the long *silence des siècles*.

Appendix

TABLE I. The Narrative Points of the Patterns

Laisse	Theme	Text
18	Prediction of Démesure (66 and 91)	*Lines 256 and 257* Vostre curages est mult pesmes e fiers: Jo me crendreie que vos vos meslisez.
44	Betrayal (66 and 91)	*Lines 583–93* Li reis serat as meillors porz de Sizer; Sa rereguarde avrat detrés sei mise; Iert i sis niés, li quens Rolland, li riches, E Oliver, en qui il tant se fiet. .XX. milie Francs unt en lur cumpaignie. De voz paiens lur enveiez .C. milie: Une bataille lur i rendent cil primes; La gent de France iert blecee e blesmie; Nel di por ço, des voz iert la martirie. Altre bataille lur livrez de meisme: De quel que seit Rollant n'estuertrat mie.
66	Absence of Charles (66)	*Lines 823 and 824* Sur tuz les altres est Carles anguissus: As porz d'Espaigne ad lesset sun nevold.

LAISSE	THEME	TEXT
84	Démesure (66)	*Lines 1059–69*

Cumpainz Rollant, l'olifan car sunez,
Si l'orrat Carles, ferat l'ost returner,
Succurrat nos li reis od sun barnet."
Respont Rollant: "Ne placet Damnedeu
Que mi parent pur mei seient blasmet
Ne France dulce ja cheet en viltet!
Einz i ferrai de Durendal asez,
Ma bone espee que ai ceint al costet:
Tut en verrez le brant ensanglentet.
Felun paien mar i sunt asemblez:
Jo vos plevis, tuz sunt a mort livrez." AOI.

| 85 | Démesure (91) | *Lines 1070–81* |

Cumpainz Rollant, sunez vostre olifan,
Si l'orrat Carles, ki est as porz passant.
Je vos plevis, ja returnerunt Franc.
—Ne placet Deu," ço li respunt Rollant,
"Que ço seit dit de nul hume vivant,
Ne pur paien, que ja seie cornant!
Ja n'en avrunt reproece mi parent.
Quant jo serai en la bataille grant
E jo ferrai e mil colps e .VII. cenz,
De Durendal verrez l'acer sanglent.
Franceis sunt bon, si ferrunt vassalment;
Ja cil d'Espaigne n'avrunt de mort guarant."

| 109 | Prediction of Trial (91) | *Lines 1406–11* |

Malvais servis le jur li rendit Guenes
Qu'en Sarraguce sa maisnee alat vendre;
Puis en perdit e sa vie e ses membres;
El plait ad Ais en fut juget a pendre,
De ses parenz ensenbl'od lui tels trente
Ki de murir nen ourent esperance. AOI.

| 110 | Prediction of Death (66) | *Lines 1423–37* |

En France en ad mult merveillus turment:
Orez i ad de tuneire e de vent,
Pluies e gresilz desmesureement;
Chiedent i fuildres e menut e suvent,
E terremoete ço i ad veirement.
De seint Michel del Peril josqu'as Seinz,
Dès Besençun tresqu'al port de Guitsand,
N'en ad recet dunt del mur ne cravent.

LAISSE	THEME	TEXT
		Cuntre midi tenebres i ad granz.

Cuntre midi tenebres i ad granz.
N'i ad clartet, se li ciels nen i fent.
Hume nel veit ki mult ne s'espoant.
Dient plusor: "Ço est li definement,
La fin del secle ki nus est en present."
Il nel sevent, ne dient vier nient:
Ço est li granz dulors por la mort de Rollant.

| 132 | Prediction of Vengeance and Burial (66) | *Lines 1742–51* |

Ja li corners ne nos avreit mester,
Mais nepurquant si est il asez melz:
Venget li reis, si nus purrat venger;
Ja cil d'Espaigne ne s'en deivent turner liez.
Nostre Franceis i descendrunt a pied,
Truverunt nos e morz e detrenchez,
Leverunt nos en bieres sur sumers,
Si nus plurrunt de doel e de pitet,
Enfuerunt nos en aitres de musters;
N'en magerunt ne lu ne porc ne chen."

| 135 | Traitor Accused (91) | *Lines 1790–95* |

Respont dux Neimes: "Baron i fait la peine!
Bataille i ad, par le men escientre.
Cil l'at traït ki vos en roevet feindre.
Adubez vos, si criez vostre enseigne,
Si sucurez vostre maisnee gente:
Asez oez que Rollant se dementet!"

| 150 | Death of Olivier (66) | *Lines 2019–21* |

Falt li le coer, le helme li embrunchet,
Trestut le cors a la tere li justet.
Morz est li quens, que plus ne se demuret.

| 176 | **Death of Roland (66 and 91)** | *Lines 2389–96* |

Sun destre guant a Deu en puroffrit.
Saint Gabriel de sa main l'ad pris.
Desur sun braz teneit le chef enclin;
Juntes ses mains est alet a sa fin.
Deus tramist sun angle Cherubin
E seint Michel del Peril;
Ensembl'od els sent Gabriel i vint.
L'anme del cunte portent en pareïs.

LAISSE	THEME	TEXT
200	Baligant Swears Vengeance (91)	*Lines 2807–9* S'or ne s'en fuit Karlemagne li veilz, Li reis Marsilie enqui sera venget: Pur sun poign destre l'en liverai le chef."
226	Charles Prays for Vengeance (91)	*Lines 3108–9* Par ta mercit, se tei plaist, me cunsent Que mun nevold poisse venger Rollant!
267	Burial (91, and 66—as laisse 198)	*Lines 3689–94* Entresqu'a Blaive ad cunduit sun nevold E Oliver, sun nobilie cumpaignun, E l'arcevesque, ki fut sages e proz. En blancs sarcous fait metre les seignurs: A Saint Romain, la gisent li baron. Francs les cumandent a Deu e a ses nuns.

TABLE 2.   The Order of Laisses Postulated for the 66 Pattern

A. To be deleted from Digby-23 as insertions by the Baligant revisionist:

Laisse 185, lines 2542–54
187–202
214–66
267, lines 3676–82
268–69
290, 291

B. Comparative order:

Digby-23	66 Pattern	Digby-23	66 Pattern	Digby-23	66 Pattern
185	185	213	197	280	209
186	186	267	198	281	210
203	187	270	199	282	211
204	188	271	200	283	212
205	189	272	201	284	213
206	190	273	202	285	214
207	191	274	203	286	215
208	192	275	204	287	216
209	193	276	205	288	217
210	194	277	206	289	218
211	195	278	207	(290) reconstructed	219
212	196	279	208	(291) reconstructed	220

Bibliography

Aebischer, Paul. *Rolandiana borealia: La saga Af Runcivals Bardaga et ses dérivés scandinaves.* Lausanne, 1954.

————. *Rolandiana et Oliveriana: Recueil d'études sur les chansons de geste.* Publications romanes et françaises, XCII. Geneva: Librairie Droz, 1967.

————. "Les trois mentions plus anciennes du couple 'Roland et Oliver,' " *Revue belge de philologie et d'histoire* 30 (1952) : 657–75.

Aristotle. *Metaphysics.* Translated by John Warrington. New York, 1956.

Augustine, Saint. *The City of God.* Translated by Marcus Dods. New York, 1950.

————. *Commentary on the Lord's Sermon on the Mount with Seventeen Related Sermons.* Translated by Dennis J. Kavanaugh. The Fathers of the Church: A New Translation, Vol. 2. New York, 1951.

————. *The Confessions and Letters of Saint Augustin, with a Sketch of his Life and Work.* Translated by Philip Schaff. A Select Library of the Nicene and Post-Nicene Fathers of the Christian Church, Vol 1. Buffalo, 1886.

Beaujouan, Guy. "Le symbolisme des nombres à l'époque romane," *Cahiers de civilisation médiévale* 4 (1961) : 159–69.

Bédier, Joseph. *Les Légendes épiques.* 4 vol. Paris, 1908–13.

Bertrand de Bar-sur-Aube. *Girart de Vienne Chanson de Geste.* Edited by F. G. Yeandle. New York, 1930.

Böklen, Ernst. *Die uglückszal Dreizehn und ihre mythische Bedeutung.* Leipzig, 1913.

Boyer, Jacques. *Histoire des mathématiques.* Paris, 1900.

Bulatkin, Eleanor Webster. "The Arithmetic Structure of the Old-French

Vie de Saint Alexis," PMLA 74 (1959) : 495–502.

Cajori, Florian. *A History of Mathematics.* New York and London, 1894.

Capella, Martianus Mineus Felix. *De nuptiis philologiae et mercurii.* Edited by Adolfus Dick. Leipzig, 1925.

Curtius, Ernst Robert. *European Literature and the Latin Middle Ages.* Translated by Willard R. Trask. New York, 1953.

——. "Zur Interpretation des Alexiusliedes," *ZRPh* 56 (1936) : 113–37.

Dante Alighieri. *La Divina Commedia.* Edited by C. H. Grandgent. Boston, London, 1933.

——. *La vita nuova.* Edited by Kenneth McKenzie. New York, 1922.

Delbouille, Maurice. *Sur la genèse de la Chanson de Roland.* Brussels, 1954.

Delehaye, Hippolyte. *Les Passions des martyrs et les genres littéraires.* Brussels, 1921.

Didron, Adolphe. *Christian Iconography: The History of Christian Art in the Middle Ages.* Translated by E. J. Millington and Margaret Stokes. 2 vols. London, 1886.

Duggan, Joseph C. "Formulaic Language in the Old-French Epic Poems *Le Siège de Barbastre* and *Beuvon de Conmarchis.*" Ph.D. dissertation, The Ohio State University, 1964.

Erman, Adolf. *The Literature of the Ancient Egyptians.* Translated by A. M. Blackman. New York, 1927.

Farbridge, Maurice H. *Studies in Biblical and Semitic Symbolism.* New York, 1923.

Fawtier, Robert. *La Chanson de Roland.* Paris, 1933.

Frappier, Jean. *Les Chansons de geste du cycle de Guillaume d'Orange.* 2 vols. Paris, 1955.

Hopper, Vincent Foster. *Medieval Number Symbolism.* New York, 1938.

Horrent, Jules. *La Chanson de Roland dans les littératures française et espagnole au moyen âge.* Paris, 1951.

Imhoff, Paul G. "The Numerical Symbolism in the Old-French Poem *La Vie de Saint Alexis,*" Master's thesis, University of Maryland, 1963.

Karls des Grossen Reise nach Jerusalem und Constantinople. Edited by Eduard Koschwitz. Leipzig, 1923.

Le Gentil, Pierre. *La Chanson de Roland.* Paris, 1955.

Li Gotti, Ettori. *La Chanson de Roland e i Normanni.* Florence, 1949.

Lejeune, Rita. "La Naissance du couple littéraire 'Roland et Olivier,'" *Mélanges Henri Grégoire,* II, in *Annuaire de l'Institut de Philologie et d'Histoire Orientales et Slaves* 10 (1950) : 372–401.

Louis, René. *Girart, comte de Vienne dans les chansons de geste.* Paris, 1947.

Lord, Albert. *The Singer of Tales.* Cambridge, Mass., 1960.

Lot, Ferdinand. "Etudes sur les légendes épiques françaises," *Romania* 54 (1928) : 357–80.

Lucas, Robert. "The Mathematical Structure of the *Chanson de Roland,* MS Digby-23." Master's thesis. The Ohio State University, 1964.

McLean, Charles Victor. *Babylonian Astrology and its Relation to the Old Testament.* Toronto, 1929.

Menéndez-Pidal, Ramón. *La Chanson de Roland et la tradition épique des Francs.* Edited by René Louis. Translated by Irénée-Marcel Cluzel. Paris, 1960.

———. *Poesia juglaresca y origenes de las literaturas romanicas.* 6th edition. Madrid, 1957.

Menninger, Karl. *Number Words and Number Symbols.* Translated by Paul Broneer. Cambridge, Mass.: M.I.T. Press, 1969.

Mireaux, Emile. *La Chanson de Roland et l'histoire de France.* Paris, 1943.

Mortier, Paul. *Les textes de la Chanson de Roland.* 10 vols. Paris, 1940.

Nicomachus of Gerasa. *Introduction to Arithmetic.* Translated by Martin Luther D'Ooge. New York, 1926.

Paris, Gaston. *La Vie de Saint Alexis, poème du XIe siècle et renouvellements des XIIe, XIIIe et XIVe siècles avec préfaces, variantes, notes et glossaire.* Paris, 1872.

Parry, Milman. *Les formules et la métrique d'Homère.* Paris, 1928.

Pauphilet, Albert. "Sur la *Chanson de Roland,*" *Romania* 59 (1933): 161–98.

Pèlerinage de Charlemagne. See *Karls des Grossen Reise nach Jerusalem und Constantinople.*

Pellegrini, S. *La Canzone di Rolando.* Milan, 1952.

Philo Judaeus. *The Allegorical Interpretation of Genesis II, III.* Philo with an English Translation, by F. H. Colson and G. H. Whitaker, Vol. 1. The Loeb Classical Library. London, 1929.

———. *The Works of Philo Judaeus, the Contemporary of Josephus.* Translated by C. D. Yonge. 4 vols. London, 1855.

Plato. *The Republic of Plato.* Translated by Benjamin Jowett. 5 vols. New York, 1892.

———. *Plato's Timaeus.* Translated by Francis M. Cornford. Edited by Oskar Piest. New York, 1929.

Plotinus. *Plotinus: Complete Works.* Edited and translated by Kenneth Sylvan Guthrie. 4 vols. London, 1918.

Plutarch. *Sur l'E de Delphes.* Edited and translated by Robert Flacelière. Annales de l'Université de Lyon, Série IIIe, fasicule II. Paris, 1941.

Proclus Diadochus. *Elements of Theology.* Translated by E. R. Dods. Oxford, 1933.

Rajna, Pio. "Contributi alla storia dell'epopea e del romanzo medievale VII: L'onomastica italiana e l'epopea carolingia," *Romania* 18 (1889): 1–69.

Riquer, Martin de. *Los Cantares de gesta franceses.* Madrid, 1952 and 1957.

Robson, C. A. "The Technique of Symmetrical Composition in Medieval Poetry." In *Studies in Medieval French Presented to Alfred Ewert,* edited by E. A. Francis. Oxford, 1961.

Rychner, Jean. *La Chanson de geste: Essai sur l'art épique du jongleur.*

Geneva, 1955.

Samaran. *La Chanson de Roland: Réproduction phototypique du manuscrit Digby-23.* Paris, 1933.

Singleton, Charles S. *An Essay on the Vita Nuova.* Cambridge, Mass.: Harvard University Press, 1949.

————. "The Poet's Number at the Center," *MLN* 80 (1965).

Smith, Henry Preserved. *Old Testament History.* New York, 1903.

Spitzer, Leo. "Etudes d'anthroponymie ancienne française," *PMLA* 58 (1943) : 589–93.

Thompson, R. Campbell. *Semitic Magic, Its Origin and Development.* London, 1908.

Van der Waerden, Bartel Leendert. *Science Awakening.* Translated by Arnold Dresden. Gröningen, 1954.

Vie de Saint Alexis, La. Edited by C. Storey. Oxford, 1946.

Webster, Hutton. *Rest Days: A Study in Early Law and Morality.* New York, 1916.

Weston, Jesse L. *The Legend of Sir Perceval.* 2 vols. London, 1906–9.

Index

398.2
B933s
59663

Bulatkin, Eleanor
Webster
Structural arithmetic
metaphor in the Oxford
"Roland"   DAY 438

398.2   59663
B933s

Bulatkin, Eleanor Webster

Structural arithmetic
metaphor in the Oxford
"Roland"

WITHDRAWN

DAVIS MEMORIAL LIBRARY

3 7110 0001 9906 1